An Onion of Wars

Books by Tony Medina

POETRY

An Onion of Wars
Broke on Ice
My Old Man Was Always on the Lam
Committed to Breathing
Sermons from the Smell of a Carcass Condemned to Begging
No Noose Is Good Noose
Emerge & See

FOR YOUNG READERS

The President Looks Like Me
I and I, Bob Marley
Follow-up Letters to Santa from Kids Who Never Got a Response
Love to Langston
Christmas Makes Me Think
DeShawn Days

AS EDITOR

Bum Rush the Page: A Def Poetry Jam (with Louis Reyes Rivera)
Role Call: A Generational Anthology of Social and Political Black Literature & Art
(with Samiya A. Bashir and Quraysh Ali Lansana)
In Defense of Mumia (with S.E. Anderson)

An Onion of Wars

TONY MEDINA

Third World Press

Progressive Black Publishing Since 1967

Chicago

Third World Press
Publishers since 1967
Chicago

Printed in the United States of America
First Edition

Cover art by Jean-Michel Basquiat
Riding with Death, 1988; Acrylic and oil paintstick on canvas
© 2012 The Estate of Jean-Michel Basquiat / ADAGP, Paris / Artists Rights
Society, New York

Library of Congress Cataloging-in-Publication Data

Medina, Tony.
   An onion of wars / by Tony Medina. — 1st ed.
     p. cm.
   ISBN 978-0-88378-330-6 (pbk. : alk. paper)
   I. Title.
   PS3563.E2414O55 2012
   811'.54—dc23   2011041888

Cover and book design by Miriam Ahmed | www.miryum.com

18 17 16 15 14 13 12   6 5 4 3 2 1
www.twpbooks.com

FOR MY AUNT, **VILMA MEDINA,** WHO RAISED ME

Contents

1   Chucha's Last Christmas

LETTERS TO SANTA

5   Francine Francis (age 13)
6   Rene Crenshaw (age 11)
7   Rodney Cheo Hampton (age 13)
8   Georgie Maldonado (age 12)
9   Eli Richardson (age 11)
11   Deidra Wilcox (age 14)
13   Lydia Muñoz (age 13)
14   Cassandra Elise Matisse (age 14)
15   Demitri Vega (age 14)
16   Samantha Negrón (age 13)
17   Barack Obama (age 50)

AN ONION OF WARS

21   Landscape with Chalk-Marked Silhouette
22   An Onion of Wars
23   Autobiography of a Welfano
25   Broke Found Poem
26   Broke Barbie
28   Quartering Time
29   Camden
30   Triptych with Star and Tulips
30   *First Suit*
31   *Star*
32   *Tulips*
33   Bread
34   Los Olvidados
35   Congo
36   Soldier the Burden
37   Gaza Stripped
38   On the Way to the Jewish Monument
39   Lebanon
40   How Much Yellow Cake

41   Oedipal Nightmares

42   Saro-Wiwa!

43   Oil's Well That Ends Well

45   The Confessor's Confession

46   Rumsfeld Confesses at a Mosque in Harlem

51   Brown Sonnet

52   The Autobiography of Michael Jackson's Skin

53   When Kong Was King

55   JB's Great Escape

57   Elvis at 75

58   Bush League

59   The Money Shot

60   Just Enough for the City

63   Being Part of the Axis of Evil

64   Bipolar Blues

65   Double-Barreled Diptych Blues

65   *Indignant Blues*

66   *Pink Slip Blues*

67   Occupy This

SOMETHING HIP HOP THIS WAY COMES

73   Bling Bling

74   Hip Hop Hurts Sometimes

77   Blue Scowl Aubade

79   Aqua Solo

80   Things to Blame Hip Hop For

83   Radio Daze

83   *Things to Hang Don Imus On*

84   *On Laura Schlessinger and Her N-Word Rant*

85   Something Hip Hop This Way Comes

87   The Keepin' It Real Awards

88   Everything You Wanted to Know about Hip Hop but Were Afraid to Be Hipped for Fear of Being Hopped

90   Twatting Around on Twitter

91   Bestseller, Required Text, the Future of Black Literature?

92   Slam-A-Lot

94   Upcoming Reality Shows

95   Books I Need to Write

SERIOUS TROUBLE WILL BYPASS YOU

99   Sisyphus Speaks
100   Atlas Shrugged
102   The Nights Are Long
104   And Winding
106   They Say He Never Knew What Hit Him
107   When I Think of You, Love
109   Serious Trouble Will Bypass You
112   In the Garden of Goods and Evils
113   Coal Miner's Slaughter
114   Cannibals on U Street
115   Questions on the Police Officer's Exam
116   Byrd on a Wire
117   Red
118   Derrion Speaks from Blood on Concrete
119   Alas Poor Richard, Not Much Has Changed
120   Dis Association
124   Kwansaba
125   Birthin' Blues by the Bayou

To tell the truth is to become beautiful.
— June Jordan

CHUCHA'S LAST CHRISTMAS

No more vacant lot eyes staring
    Blankly into your future

You used to dream of being a dancer
    Of letting your heart move

Along your *nalgas*
    Along the island of your pulse

O what rhythms wrestled through
    Veins of heroin & coke

& frustrated despair
    Of being a Black Puerto Rican

Woman, *una negra* unsatisfied
    In her captive world

How you wanted to merengue the
    Shit out of those motherfuckers

& let 'em know what it be's like
    Chucha, there are no more long nights

In welfare hotels
    No more selling dreams at the OTB

Or lifetimes & lifetimes spent in a bottle
    Dangling between a needle & a vein

No more lives & times & dreams & pains
    Rolled up in Bambu paper

You used to walk those winter nights
    Alone stone cold in your salsa blues

Your wetness turning to icicles in your
    Drawers, dreaming of eating *pasteles*

In your grandma's house
    Those days are over now, Chucha

Who was to know that you would hug
    The third rail & who could blame you?

Letters to Santa

Sometimes I dream that
I lived somewhere else

Dear Santa,

I'm writing you because I'm sad.
My older sister got AIDS from a needle
when she used to do drugs.
I can't stand to see her suffer.
She is always in so much pain.
My mother had to take off from
work to take care of her because
she's always either sick in the bed
with diarhea and numonia or
going to the hospital because she
don't eat or could hardly breathe.

My mother almost got fired from her
job because she took so many days
off from work to take care of her.
Sometimes I leave school early
so I could be there to help her
clean up or go to the bathroom.
I try to cook her things she could eat
without getting tired or throwing up
all the time like she does.

What I'm asking for is nothing for me
but for my sister and mother.
We need money to be able to take her
to a better hospital cause
the one she go to is too dirty
and crowded and it take too
long for the doctor to help.
Plus the medicine is too much
money and my mother could
hardly afford it.

If you send the money
to help us, I promise
when I get out of school
and get a job we'll pay you
back.

RENE CRENSHAW (AGE 11)
MALCOLM X BLVD, HARLEM, NY

Dear Santa Clause,

Im writing you cause
I wanted to tell you
about what I did
last spring with my
mother when we went
on a bus trip to
where the president lives
to bring letters to Janet
Jackson Reno
for mumia abjamal
who went to jail
for telling the truth
about the govament
we was marching and I
was handing out flyers
to people to help
save him cause
they want to kill
him in the alectrick chair
because he fight
for black people
like me.

Santa I know you are very very
busy because you would of been
there with me with your
raindears and sled helping me
hand out flyers. Plus you would
of had alot of fun on the bus
because we was singing and
saying poems and playing
the drums. And your sled
could of been on top of the bus to.

So please help save mumia
and black people
from the govament.

From Rene Crenshaw
from Harlem

RODNEY CHEO HAMPTON (AGE 13)
BROWNSVILLE, BROOKLYN, NY

Dear Santa,

The cops make me hate them.
There mostly white but there
are some black ones too
I don't like either. They be
shootin people in the back
like they did my brother when
he didn't even have a gun
and wasn't doing nothin but
playing dice in front of the building
And they don't even get in trouble
for killing black people and
puerto ricans neither.
They don't even know how me and
my mother and father was crying
and my grandmother too. They had
to take her out the funeral because
she was falling down crying
and they ended up taking her
to the hospital because of her
heart. Then we would of been
going to two funerals. I really
would of died.

Anyway, the other day our teacher asked us
what we wanted to be when we
grow up. And my friend Jason
said to our teacher he wanted to be
guess what? Yep a cop. But I told
him I might have to shoot him
because I don't like cops. And then
I got in trouble when the teacher
heard that. But I don't care
because when I grow up
I'm never going to be one.
In fact that's why I want
a gun to shoot the cop
that killed my brother.
Do you think that's a
bad thing to ask for?

Love, Cheo

GEORGIE MALDONADO (AGE 12)
E. 6TH ST. AND AVE. B, NYC

Dear Santa,

I was born in jail.
That's what I just fount out.
This boy name Ricky in my class
kept bothering me. He said my
mother was a hoe and a crackhead
and that's why I don't have a
real mother. And then I beat him
up until the teacher was yelling
at me and sent me to the principals
office. I told my mother but she said
everything was true. She's not my
real mother and she don't know
where she's at. And I was only
writing you to help me find my
real mother. But I know you
didn't answer my other letter
and maybe you wont answer
this one since I punched Ricky
in his face. But he started with
me first.

Love,
Georgie

ELI RICHARDSON (AGE 11)
GARY, INDIANA

Dear Santa,

I don't know if you
would listen to me
or not because I have
to lie alot. But I don't
lie on purpose. I only
lie because I don't want
my mother to get in trouble.

But one time when I was
taking my coat off to hang
up in the closet in school
my teacher saw a scar
on my back and then she saw
other bruises I had and asked me
where they came from and
I said I fell when I was playing
in the big park with my cousin
Jameson. But I don't think she
believed me.

And then when I got home
my mother beat me again
for telling my teacher.
She said the teacher was trying
to get the welfare to take me
away. She said if I run and tell
the teacher she would go to jail.

But sometimes I hope she do
go to jail because even though
she say she don't mean it after
she still always gets mad at me
for doing something or yells
at me and hits me with the belt
or a broom or pinches and
punches me too. Sometimes
she even hits me in front
of alot of people. One time

9

she beat me in front of the
building. And another time
she hit me with a hanger
and the plug that connects
to the TV and she threw
the iron at me and said
I was good for nothing
and that I was going to be
just like my father.
But the iron didn't burn me
because I was behind
the big chair in the livinroom.

Sometimes I dream that
I lived somewhere else and
that she was not my mother.
And other times I dream
she was nicer to me and
happier like other peoples
mothers.

Maybe you could help her
to not get mad all the time
and to not hit me anymore
because it hurts me and
gives me alot of bruises.
Thats why I don't like to
wear short sleeve shirts
because I'm embarassed
that somebody might see.

And maybe if she change
and get better I don't
have to lie anymore
because I'm scared
she might go to jail.

Yours truly,
Eli

DEIDRA WILCOX (AGE 14)
OKLAHOMA CITY, OKLAHOMA

Dear Santa Claus,

In class the other day
we all did collages to
send to the parents
of the kids who were
killed in the Oklahoma
City bombing. My sister's
friend knew somebody
there who was killed
in the bombing. How do
people get those bombs?
Why do they use them
to blow people up
especially innocent kids?
I think people who kill
kids like that are psychos.
I wonder if they think about how
those kids felt and how
their parents feel. Sometimes
I think what if that was me
and I was stuck in a building
that got blown up and then
I died because I couldn't
breathe or a piece
of the building fell on me
and smashed me like a roach.
I wonder what my mother
would think. She would
probably die if something
happened to me like that.

It would be nice if every
body would take time
out once a week to send
nice letters to each other
instead of blowing people
up or killing people.

I don't want anything
for me this christmas.
I just want there to be
peace on earth,
no more wars and
violence like you see
on TV all the time
and for every body
to hug at least once
a day and feel good
about themselves and
help each other instead
of hurting each other
like we do all the time.
Why don't people just
do something for somebody
else for a change like feed
the homeless once a week.
Hopefully there won't be
no more suffering like
there was in Oklahoma City.
I would ask for a wish that
would be about the bomber
and how he should rot in jail
and burn in hell. But maybe
he needs to be educated by
the letters that we're sending
in our collage. But if I was
to have just one wish maybe
it should be that the bombing
never took place in the first
place and those babies were
back where they belong
at home with there parents
enjoying christmas and writing
letters to Santa Claus.

Love always,
Deidra

Dear Santa,

My mother and father came here
when I was five years old from
Mexico. My father works on a
farm in California where he
has to pick grapes all day
that are sprayed with chemicals
to kill the bugs that get on them.
And he's been getting sick alot
lately because of it. The doctor
at the clinic that he goes to
said it might be related to
the spray that they use and
that he should sue the company
he works for because they knew
how bad those chemicals were for
people. But my father is scared
he might lose his job because he
still doesn't have his citizenship
and he might get deported by
immigration. And my mother
argues with him alot about it
because she hates to see him
suffer like that and she's
worried something might
happen to him and we won't
have him to take care of us.
He wakes up tired and coughing
and he always has these bad
headaches and he never has
time or energy to take me nowhere
like he use to. And he doesn't
take the doctor's advice and still
goes to work every day because
he has to take care of his family.
But what will happen to us if
god forbid he dies?

CASSANDRA ELISE MATISSE (AGE 14)
CHICAGO, ILLINOIS

Dear Santa,

I'm helping my brother Eric
send letters to people to warn
them about "The Mountain"
where we live. "The Mountain"
is where this guy let all these companies
put poisonous chemicals that
pollute the air and give people
cancer in our neighborhood.
In the letters we say how he used to
let people dump chemicals near us
for 120 dollars and then brung the
price down to only 6 dollars. And
then now all of these companies
started coming and dumping there
chemicals here. And with these
letters we're trying to educate
people about the dumpsite in
our neighborhood so they could
help us try and stop him letting
people dump their chemicals
here. Because one of our next
door neighbors just found out
that they got cancer and some
women who were pregnant
gave birth to babies with
birth defects and lukemia.
These innocent babies were
born deformed and sick with
cancer. This gets me motivated
to help my older brother send
out these letters and get people
to sign petitions against this guy.
I just wanted to let you know
that I now know how you must
feel writing all those letters
because it is very tiring. Also
please help us get rid of this
guy and put him away in jail
where he belongs for the rest
of his life. Or maybe better
yet let them move that
dumpsite to where he lives.

Sincerely yours,
Cassandra

Dear Santa,

I wish I had the money to buy
flowers to send to all the parents
whose children were killed by
that guy with the four guns
in that gym in Scottland.
I would wish that he dies
but he's already dead.
Why do you think he hated
children like that? Anyway
I think they should ban weapons
and keep them away from people.
Guns are too dangerous because
people can't be trusted. Not
even cops because even when
there not working they carry
there guns and some of them
even shoot people or shoot
themselves when they get
drunk. Well maybe I don't
just want money to send flowers
to those parents and teachers
in Scottland. Maybe it would
just be easier to stop people
from getting guns.

Dear Santa,

I hate my teacher because she got
my friend Sonia kicked out
of our school because she said she
was a illegal alien and that the
govament told her to squeal
or tattle tail on people who
dont got there green card.
She said the classroom
was over crowded anyway.
But that doesn't mean that
kids like Sonia shouldn't
get an education. I wish
I didn't have a teacher like her
because I think she's
prejudice and racist and
also because of her big mouth
I lost my best friend.
Please bring Sonia back
and get rid of her instead,
huh Santa?

BARACK OBAMA (AGE 50)
THE WHITE HOUSE, WASHINGTON, DC

Dear Santa,

These Tea Party mofos are drivin' me crazy.
I'm about to get black on those dumbass in-bred
hillbilly motherfuckers.

Got my hair all gray. Have me eatin' nasty, greazy-ass
beef burgers and pork sammiches. Soon I'll be
poppin' Viagara like Tic Tacs, with high blood and sugar.

They don't want nobody to get healthcare—
not even they mama. You should see some
of these motherfuckers teefuses—you would think
they was from England.

In their mind up is down and down is where
they wanna keep the black half of my ass.
They lie about me constantly and see my tie
as a noose they'd like to hook to the back of a pickup truck
doin' 90 from The White House.

They don't wanna ever acknowledge that half of me
is whiter than their dingy-ass drawers.
They don't want to tax the rich, even though
a lot of those tea toking sheep humpers are poor as rabbit shit.

These hatin' mofos can't stand the fact that
Me and Michelle be wearin' out that Lincoln bedroom.
Make me wanna grab my nuts at them savages
and be like, *Oh skeet skeet skeet skeet skeet skeet!* [LMBAO]

Anyway, you know that line from Richard Pryor
where he's actin' like a black preacher in *The Exorcist*;
where Linda Blair plays a little girl possessed by
The Devil and the black preacher, signifyin' The Devil
is a pedophile, makes a call to heaven and says: *Dear God,
The Devil's a low motherfucker—Can you exorcise his ass to Cleveland?*

Well, Santa, *can* you?

An Onion of Wars

*How hard to remember
a time without shooting*

LANDSCAPE WITH CHALK-MARKED SILHOUETTE

for Gwendolyn Brooks

They real dope. They
Like to smoke. They

Crack some .40s. They
Hit the shorties. They

Hang on the Ave. They
Loves to laugh. They

Shoot C-Lo in the hall. They
Drive-by the mall. They

Play some B-ball. They
Love to shoot hoops. They

Sit on front stoops. They
Watch the girlies go by. They

Bullshit and tell lies. They
Like to stay high. They

Don't ever wanna die. They
Make they mama cry. They

Sit on front stoops. They
Waste a lot of time. They

Watch planes go by.
Planes go by.

Within this war
   Is another war

Within that war
   Another war unfolds

Twin towers
   Of war

Collapsing &
   Coagulating

Into a union
   Of wars

Within those wars
   Is a labyrinth

Of wars
   Within that house of wars

A maze of wars
   Erected like

A Rubik's Cube
   Of wars

Within all these wars
   The splitting of flesh

The shattering of bones
   Blood splatter

On a yellow dress
   An empty swing

Creaking in the wind
   The stench

Of indifference
   Screams followed by silence

Shrapnel pock-marking the sky
   Smoke stabbing at the eyes

Yo soy el hombre que respira debajo del agua!
—Héctor Lavoe

I am from heroin needles
    In the open sore
        Dry humps beneath a staircase
    Pissy & drunk
Nodding out in a string
    Of vomit
        The sun tap dancing
    On broken glass

The streets with twinkles
    In its eyes
        I am from rice & beans
    & platanos
From Shangó Elégba
    & batá drum
        From candles & incense
    & prayers by the window

Dreaming of numbers
    Coming out for Brooklyn
        Rent parties & slow drags
    Brown tamarindo lindo
With the African nose
    & Indian hair
        I am from palm trees
    In the hulls of ships

Arthritic knees from
    Concrete kiss
        Beneath hopscotch feet
    & skelzie schemes
I am from fathers on the lam
    & mothers glazed like ham
        I am from yucca & yams
    From collard greens pork grind loins

& domino scenes
From piragua carts
& coquito screams
From Salsa Plena
To bango Boogaloo
Hustler break dance beats
I am from kinky curly afro crowns
Ornery halos of bandana flags

Saluted above handlebar
Mustache frowns
I am what's left from running
The streets
Unexpected sperm
In the sheets
The byproduct
Of music of rum

& how it makes you
Horny
Of salsa & sun
& shit confined to
Languages that are corny
I resist the temptation
To be plain to be sane
Enough to be put in my place

My laughter & hips
Invade Space
I am from Africa Yorùbá Taíno
Moorish divide
I glide through continents of time
Divided by doubt self-worry
& pride
Denied

I am from the first
& everlasting stride
Survival eternal
Resistance is where I reside

Police say
      A motorcyclist

Dead set against
      Wearing a helmet

Participating in a
      Protest ride

Against helmet laws
      In upstate New York

Died after he flipped
      Over the handlebars

And hit his head
      On the pavement

BROKE BARBIE

Lives in the cardboard box
She came in

Not a Mattel original
Straight off the show-

Room floor
But a factory flung

Bland broken
Down generic one

Face weather-beaten
& worn, her once

Bright smile whittled
Down by the sadness

Of hunger & time
Hair matted

Feet dirty & covered
In tiny black

Disposable
Garbage bags

This Barbie
Been through a lot

This Barbie
Walks the streets

Roams through
Tiny trash bins

In search of meals
This Barbie does not

Have a price tag or a seal
Her cold plastic rubbery skin

Has a grimy film
Like a dirty eraser

You rub to make
Clean again

Her Ken left her
For a crack pipe

So small
You could barely

Hold it with
Two fingers

This Barbie's mama
Put her out

A long time ago
For not doing

What she said
For staying out

All hours
Of the night

For dropping out of school
For getting knocked up

For aborting twins
For cursing & fighting

For insisting her stepfather
Touched her

How the baby is released from the womb:
Bullwhip's quick slash fanfare confetti of flesh;
Fear's awestruck parted red sea lips in full bloom,

Raw thunderous silent stillborn eruption;
Hate's crude scalpel sting, its serpent's steel tongue
Lash, cruelty's vile measured laceration—

Mangled scar tissue cradle of blood, a cargo ship
Weighted with the burden of memory
Precious as freedom's neglected postscript

Inscribed in the quartered mother's wounded
Womb. How a baby enters the world, plucked
Fledgling from its nest, with ravenous intent—

Red clay cracked in the eye of the sun: minced
Flower of tender flesh pushed through to loom
Arrested from the belly of its tomb.

CAMDEN

Moochie
in a garden
of needles
food stamp fed
alcoholic battle zone home
six-pack of beer
half-a-pint of Vodka a day.
*So messed up so
messed up*...Daddy says.
Please stop drinking...Mommie says.
I love you, Moochie...Daddy says.
The picture you draw,
Mom and Dad holding hands.
*All you do is drink drink
drink... What kind of father figure
are you? You don't help me
with the bills... You're an
alcoholic!* Mommie screaming
at the top of her lungs.
When they argue I get headaches,
like this, she says, snapping
her fingers.
            What do you dream about?
the doctor asks my dad.
*Hanging myself. Throwing
myself out the window.*
            But I don't have the courage.
I'm scared about my dad,
throw a kiss to him.
He looks sad behind
the window of the rehab.
            *You think he'll be
alright there?*
Moochie asks her mom.
She just sits and
looks past her.
In the park
she is tour guide
six going on sixty
she knows this
landscape well
matter-of-factly turns to
the camera's lens, *Watch out!
This is where the drug dealers
plant their needles.*

First Suit

The police officers carried the small
Suit, as if it were my son, lifeless, in outstretched
    Arms. I remember the funeral director
Asking me for a suit to bury him in.

But he was so young—he had nothing formal
To wear—I couldn't bear the thought of buying
    My son's first suit worn for his casket.
And so the officers who responded to our call

Chipped in to purchase it, as if they were buying
Flowers. At the wake he looked peaceful and sharp
    As a tack—not with that last look of anguish—how
My tears drenched his face—I could feel the pain as
    His sickle cell spleen ballooned and burst in his frail
Body—all eight years of him, stuck in a lifetime's suit.

Star

Hey Daddy, how do I look? I hope Mom don't
Cry. She always makes a big deal of stuff.
    Like the time I rode my bike without training
Wheels, or when I was a tree in the forest

    In my first grade class. Remember how she made
A cake and invited everybody
    Over like it was my birthday? I felt like
A star the way everybody was fussing

    Over me and all I was was a tree.
But that made me want to be in more plays and
    In movies and on TV so you and Mom
Would be proud of me. I wanted her to
    See me in a suit but not like this one. Please
Don't let her see me in this little old box.

Tulips

I thought it was a toy, the girl said, clutching
The caved-in scar on the left side of her head,
    Planted by a cluster bomb sticking out the mud.
When I picked it up it blew up in my ear.

    I couldn't hear anything but a ringing
Sound that only I could hear; everything was quiet.
    People were screaming but I could not hear.
I looked over to my sister who was crying;

    Blood was all over her white dress like she got
Sprayed with a water gun—but she wasn't wounded
    At all. When she finally got up, a piece
Of my skull fell out of her dress like a cut flower.
    That's when I noticed my head like a flowerpot
Sprouting blood and bits of flesh like red tulips.

BREAD

Not too far to go in a land without bread
Children flock like pigeons after bullets of bread

Janjaweed shout commands and pockmark sand
At children that pluck through sand for bread

How hard to remember a time without shooting,
A time without shooing, hiding behind Ma-Ma for bread

That came natural as breast milk with its endless spring
But now what is sucked are bullet casings resembling bits of bread

Or peanut shells in this desert hell deserted by parents
Unable to escape the long beak of death hungry for bread

What cracks the air is what cracks the tiny skull
Snapped and split like the snapping stick of bread

Leaking from a clear hole in the skull
Blood gets sucked by each grain porous as bread

And from that cracked teapot skull what one sees:
Light trickling through a cobweb of bread

LOS OLVIDADOS

We begged for table scraps so long we could barely manage
Breadcrumbs too large for our backs to carry

Over borders and into the folds of cardboard boxes
Simple raindrops became tsunamis

A breeze would snatch our life away
Before you knew it they wanted us to pay for air and water

The chores became so unbearable chiropractors adjusted
Our ribcages like wooden beads on an abacus

In order to weigh the plus and minuses of our despair
They held us in the palms of their hands and shook us

Lightly like dice careened into corners, stars twirling
Just above our heads like electric dust mites

We came up sixes instead of sevens
We knew our luck ran out when they put us back in their pockets

And we got lost among some loose change and dirty lint
Balanced at the edge of a hole small enough to trap flies

The men in uniform
    Scorch our village
Hack our limbs off

    Like sugarcane
The men in uniform
    Ram their bodies

Into ours
    Jab the butts
Of their weapons

    Into our seams
Their laughter
    Drowns out

Our screams
    Rain will not
Put out the flames

    Sunlight will not
Reveal their names
    The men in uniform

Split open our wombs
    Then move on to
Other wounds

SOLDIER THE BURDEN

Will a roadside bomb make confetti of my flesh
Will a hand grenade scramble my brains
Will Molotov cocktail flames cling to each pore
Will my skin evaporate in the wind
Will there be a yard sale for my limbs
Will a little girl's splattered blood cleanse me of sin

— Soldier contemplating uncertainty of future.

— Brazen, direct, to the point.
— fears magnified by & their most vivid visualisation.

Paradise comes in bits and pieces, strips peeled
From the flesh of olive trees, coarse as sand in veins.
Scentless gas bombs like ghost hands weld eyes and mouths sealed.
The sky is a vast coffin lid of bloodstains.

Trees older than death ripped out like clumps of hair.
Gray buildings bulldozed while children sleep and pray,
Scatter like pigeons into a lion's lair,
Trapped in a place where not even God could stay.

What rises from the earth, pockmarked through concrete,
Cannot be chewed up and spit out by tank teeth;
Will not be mashed down by the steel heel of defeat.
Faith, once crucified, emerges from the heath.

Hope found in stones thrown at the blank stares of walls.
Black smoke of anguish clouds the land where peace falls.

ON THE WAY TO THE JEWISH MONUMENT

for Lesley-Ann Brown

In Berlin
   I walk among
The gypsy ghosts of Jews
   A wailing trailing from
The leather soles of shoes

   The fable of history
Laid out like a table
   Amidst ruins
Where the natives
   Ride bikes

Dodging tourists
   Hidden behind maps
Lost in a labyrinth
   Of garish gothic buildings
And claustrophobic balconies

   Staring down at the
Black cobblestone eyes
   Of streets that once
Curbed Jews carted
   Off to crematoria

LEBANON

I would like my blood to stay where it is
I'm used to the smooth of my skin

I would hate for it to be
Burned off my bones by the blast

Of a bomb or the split brick of my house
Collapsed like a heart clogged with fury

HOW MUCH YELLOW CAKE

How much yellow cake uranium
Does it take to impeach a president

How many forged documents
To screw in a light bulb

How much oil does it take to
Grease the ass of the middle class

How much bullshit to loosen
The bowels of media manipulation

And political pundits on the payrolls
Of war companies

How many lies does it take
To notice the flies

How many Hail Marys Full of Grace
To disgrace Jesus and the intelligent

How many Supreme Court nominees
Does it take to play Kick the Klan

How many condoms to a Leezza
How many scabby knees to a skeeze-uh

How many colons to a Powell
How many necks yet to squeeza

How many body parts to a freezer
How many nutsacks to a sleeze-uh

How much anthrax to a sneeze-uh
How many bombs bursting in air to a wheeze-uh

How many psychos to a path
How many burials to each nation

How many cains to dis able
How many monuments to death

How much worship is there left

I'm Against the War
    I'm for the Troops
I'm Against Slavery
    I'm for the Overseers
I'm Against Imperialism
    I'm for the Agents of Imperial Rule
I'm Against Colonialism
    I'm for My Colonizer who Gives Good Colonoscopies
I'm Against the Genocide of Native Americans
    I'm for Andrew Jackson Indian Killers
I'm Against Nazi Germany
    I'm for Seig Heil Goosestepping Right-Wing Nazis
I'm Against Getting My Ass Beat
    I'm for the Motherfucker Who's Beatin' My Ass
I'm Against a Full Frontal Lobotomy
    My Aunt Looks Like Nurse Ratchet
I'm Against Being Put in a Straitjacket
    I Always Rely on the Kindness of Strangers
I'm Against Oedipus and the Notion of Killing My Pops and
   Sleeping with My Moms
    What Up Yo, Back in the Day I Used to Walk with a Limp
I'm Against Videos of Ho's Ass Flappin' G-Sring Snappin'
    Hey, If They Wanna Take Off Their Clothes
I'm Against the Wholesale Slaughter of Porky the Pig
    Yo, Bacon Smells Gooda Than a Muhfucka—and Fried
   Pork Chops is the Shit
I'm Against Death
    I Find Myself Sympathizing with The Grim Reaper
I Don't Like the Flames of Hell
    I Can See The Devil's Point

What color blood do these vampires suck
When their appetite causes hysteria
U.S. green   The color of a Shell truck
Black like the oil that chokes Nigeria

What kind of blood do these vampires rescind
When their white teeth break the necks of writers
Hanged in pools of blood wounded like the wind
Yet never breaks freedom or her fighters

What amount of blood do these vampires want
The blind scale of justice minus the truth
Land locked in the belly of a gas tank
Blood refineries with no other use

Corporate power's calculated greed
Always taking what the people need

OIL'S WELL THAT ENDS WELL

The road not taken
  Ham on rye
Spaghetti with bacon
  Bits of brain matter
Chicken soup for the sole
  Angry as dog shit
In the teeth of a shoe
  Blood splatter on a wedding dress
The Gaza Strip
  A pink slip
The emperor has no clothes
  The empire survives on bones
Oil wells in each pore
  Put the needle in the open sore
Uncle Fester
  Chester the Molester
All's well that rots & smells
  Capitalism regurgitates everything it eats
Stirred not shaken
  Iodine bottles
Skull & Crossbones
  A fascist statement
Dressed in bad ideas
  Christianity
Insanity
  The reason why you perm your hair
Bitch better have my money
  Land of milk & honey
Jump in the land o' lakes
  If a tree falls in the forest
The sound of one hand clapping
  Butt cheeks a-flapping
3D g-string
  A flag wedged up the ass
Upside down question mark stuck in a W
  The President's a McDonald's hand puppet
The First Lady a blow-up doll
  Of shock & awe
Always relying on the cum stains of strangers
  Blanche Dubois

Supine in a semi-coma
    A semicolon
Unable to make a decision
    Wishy-washy
Fluctuation stains
    Skid marks on the chin
Hairy shins
    Bombs burst in
A cracked skull
    A soup bowl
Two scoops of memory
    A dash of despair
Devil may care
    Salad tossers of Sodom

If I were a woman I'd pee standing up
    On every street grater in New York
Giving Marilyn Monroe a run for her money cup

I'd say, *Honey—you ain't seen nothing yet!*
    Then jump on the hood of the first car I see,
Pull up my lime green yellow-trimmed dress like a net

Over my head and sing like Ethel Merman—
    I have a pair of blue cotton blooms & a widow's streak
Wedged up in my cheeks—take a peek, take a peek!

RUMSFELD CONFESSES AT A MOSQUE IN HARLEM

I

Tinsel Clown

Although I don't usually admit it
   I'm a closet fan of Barry Manilow
Liberace, Jim Nabors &
   Pathmark cheeses. Sometimes, when I'm
Feeling frisky, I stalk the lingerie aisles
   Of Bloomingdales or Victoria Secrets
Running my sweaty palms along the

   Lower backs of mannequins in
Glow-in-the-dark lace tinsel tasseled things.
   I fancy myself a latter-day
J. Edgar Hoover in red satin
   Pumps & purple lamé—a devil in a blue dress
Clarence Thomas ain't got shit
   On these hairy hips!

II

I hate it when they call me Rummy.

III

Viagra Falls

I always wanted the kind of girl
That stalked me in my sleep
With a tall glass of champagne thigh
& a lemon slice of thong

I always wanted the kind of girl
That would obliterate Viagara from
Stock market scales &
CVS pharmacy shelves

I always wanted a girl that could sail
From my mind to my bed at any given time
Who could rhyme who could rhyme
As she stepped to my mic, amplifying the

Ecstatic operatic *Figaro! Figaro! Figaro!*
In me like an early morning shower
Of steaming hot water & Irish Spring

I always wanted a girl I could take home
To Mama in her birthday pajamas
A girl who'd drool with glazed donut eyes
While she navel gazed in front of the telly

Instead I get someone who grates
On my nerves with a squeaking,
Fingernails-across-the-chalkboard
Voice of insecurity & paranoia

Don't get me wrong, I don't need
A girl who's Martha Stewart, Julia Childs,
Wolfgang Puck or Chef Boyardee

But somebody slipped me a
Blow-up doll whose head is like a sieve
Who agrees with all my vile pornographic pleas
Who lives life on her hands & knees

Oh please, oh please, don't send me
A Republican a Democrat a Libertarian
A librarian a shithead or a flake

Don't send me Condoleezza Rice
With weapons of mass destruction
Smeared over her red white & blue
Black tits & pitchfork thighs

I want someone familiar with
My little white lies

IV

Barney's Drawers

If I were on a Reality TV show
I'd be sure to perambulate
Among the raw quartered bovine
Screaming bloody murder
From the mouths of freezers
Like wounded soldiers in a foxhole
Climb onto the frozen foods bin

Obliterate each fancy schmancy
Name brand individually wrapped
Lump of pasteurized cheese with my
Grandmother's false teeth
Gyrate in purple Barney drawers
Violently hump the refrigerated
Supermarket atmospheric pressure

Crawling along my jaw
Until I got sick & shit my drawers
Until I was beat down by nightsticks
Of the nightshift security crew
Dragged out like Blanche DuBois
By the paramedics, always relying on
The kindness of strangers

V

Allergies, Apologies,
Nah Son, Suck on These

I can't talk about peace without crying
Non-violent resolutions make my eyes itch
I'm allergic to reason
The only logic I know comes from
The rude end of a big stick
The barrel of a gun

We Bombed in Baghdad
Should be the condolence
In the program at my wake
My tombstone'll read like a mandate:
>*Grim & Pallbear it!*

Can this really be
Why I get the big bucks
Bringing video games to life?

Where are my glass slippers?
Who will drink out of them
Once my clawed, corn-on-the-cob
Hamhock bunioned feet are
Sandblasted free of them

This is what I contemplate
At night of late
>The taste of her skin
>Clothes I took from the dead
Songs that remind me of junior high

"God Bless America"
"Born on the Fourth of July"
>*Don't cry, dry your eye…*
Don't push me 'cause I'm close
>*To the edge, I'm tryin' not to lose*
My head…it's like a jungle
>*Sometimes it makes me wonder*
How I keep from going under—
>*Huh huh-huh huh huh-huh*

Where does it come from
This hunger to masticate
The shins of A-rab elementary
School girls?

When I had the chickenpox
I rolled them in my blanky &
Sent them to the last reservation
    Standing

Would you have loved me
More or less had I kept them
    To myself?

I care I share
I know what it's like
    To go without

Hell, the china in my grandmother's
Cupboards was made out
Of Styrofoam & plastic
    I have feelings
        I hurt

The last words my mother said to me
After she polished off her last
Bottle of O.E. was:
    I'm drinking to blot you out!

Then:
        Where's my jockstrap?
        Where's my jockstrap?

Before she keeled over
    Face first into a puddle
        Of her own vomit

Can this really be my life?
    Where are my glass slippers?
    Where are my glass slippers?

You know
    In our house
        We were never with clothes

BROWN SONNET

The music is inescapable
Pomade gleaming in a pompadour
Slicked back like a three-legged table
Of hot peas & butter, or something new—
The funk & wagnals of The Empire
Denying its progeny of despair
Of chain gang blues & slave ship ire
The wailing caught in the whip's glaring air
Each split bleeding the sin of skin
Gospel caught in throat like cotton & gin
Each split glide & jerk of JB's scream is kin
Branding iron tattooed to flesh like kiln
Microphone stand a cross to break or bear
Drum inescapable as blood in the ear

THE AUTOBIOGRAPHY OF MICHAEL JACKSON'S SKIN

How do you go from black to white in one spin
Crotch-grabbing moonwalk atop an auction block
Defying physics, gravity, DNA
Fame: the whip's lash that thins your gin, strips your skin

I belonged to a poor pure boy black as kin
Whose nose Napoleon tore off in Egypt
Replacing it with Kirk Douglas' cleft chin
How you go from black to white to black again

Longing for tender white flesh, the standard sin
History's blanched erasure bargain basement bin:
Money, race, self-hate, invisibility—
I want to sing through such translucency

Scream back from my old brown self, precious cargo
Spinning, sing to him, *Where did our love go?*

I'm going to jump off
The Empire State Building,
flat on my face.
　　　　　—Barry Bonds

When Kong was King
Pimp smacking planes
Out the sky from atop
The Empire State Building

Nobody accused him
Of injecting
Anabolic steroids
Into his hairy belly

They didn't mind him
Crushing cars like beer cans
Flinging them like dead cicada scab
Government surplus cheese pizzas

When Kong was King
He had white women
Eating out the palm
Of his hand

His ego a helium balloon
That would never land
His power turned
White men green

Made them shit
Their drawers
With fear & awe
With shock & twisted jaw

& when he tap danced
Or hit a high note
Twirling in the air
With sax & orange ball

Grabbing his crotch &
Spinning on his head
To a broke blues beat
Scratching sound out of vinyl

Packing pain in quatrains
White men got drunk &
Thought of branches
& trees

Their eyes
Filled
With the crosshairs
Of burning flames

Perplexed puzzled &
Strained with disdain
They whined & babbled
Furiously

On AM radio
On right-wing TV
In the halls
Of Congress

As Kong pirouetted
Effortlessly
Gracefully
On red graveyard green

Sinking their white balls
Into the 14th hole
Smacking their white balls
Over gloves & walls & skulls

JB'S GREAT ESCAPE

I was born with a conk
I threw a clef note

In honky tonk
Bashed it over the head

With a monkey wrench
Like it stole something

From me
Africa all over my face

I brought it back
In style

Mama said it wasn't
Gonna be easy

Doing splits on a bed of nails
In hot spotlights

With my hair all greazy
On the deck of Desire

Sinking like the Titanic
She knew I'd shine

Knew I'd swim on
While sharks dined

On white trash bones
Like Elvis on

The toilet choking
On some

Chicken wings
Laced with coke

And phenol barbital
Dreams

I said
I'm about to do

My thang!
That's when the bass

Kicked in
Slapped him upside

His head
Until he nodded off

And fell in his own
Vomit

Face first
As if in snow

You can't be
Sittin' up on no

Toilet takin'
A shit stealin'

My shit
I know that's the

American way
But hey

Like I say
Baybehbaybehbaybeh

Baybehbaybehbaybeh
Baybehbaybehbaybeh

Maceo!
   Where's

      My
        Cape

Who would've thought that
Hip replacement surgery
Would give me a shot

In the arm
That it would take me back
To those herky-jerky

Gyrating Ed Sullivan days
Only this time I wouldn't be
Shot from the chest up

But be a sensation on Youtube
And early morning shows
Giving old ladies something

To wrap their dentures around
Besides coffee-dunked French bread
My classic signature snarl

Preserved uplifted
And rebooted by liposuction Botox
And battery operated plastic surgery

My pompadour waxed and unwrapped
With its streaks of gray gleaming
In studio lights   crystal meth holding

My gut at bay behind guitar hands
Swinging ecstatically like a hound dog
In blue suede shoes

Like a convict breaking jailhouse rocks
Toilet paper clinging to my heels
Reignited like a wind-flapped flag

Staking its claim again
In the black ass of the rhythm
And the blues

BUSH LEAGUE

Probably never stuck
Their eight-year-old tongues
Out at the cold stab
Of late autumn rain

Or made snow angels
On their backs
Staring at a glistening
Black lake of stars

Spent childhood summers
Chasing down squirrels
Out of trees with
Heavy rocks

Stuffing live frogs with
Firecrackers after
Weighing their soft wet
Bellies down with salt

Burning unsuspecting ants with
Magnifying glasses
Torturing roaches caught in the grip
Of hairspray flame rings

In a tsunami flush
Of American Standard toilet bowls
Running off pelting stray dogs with
Empty soda bottles like roadside bombs

All this leading to a
Middle age of kids
Hooked on exploding
Television screens

Their wives in the upstairs
Bedroom feigning sleep
While down in their basements
They hunch over laptops

Addicted to porn

A close-up to the head, the unexpected
Dread—*Oh skeetskeetskeet* surprise to the forehead
To the brow to the eyes, the insult to
Injury. There are sweet half-moon arches in

The eyes. There is a crack in the smile deep as a
Scar, what fits in the groove, something resembling
Hair extensions glue, a bullwhip beating down
On you, arched & full of white brutality,

A coming together of sadness &
Cruelty, for a few dollars more, a cesspool
To store slave master fantasies—grin like a
Gracious commode, celluloid dreamscape whose

Pain runs deeper than any river passing
Through broken dolls with many holes to fill.

Dirty needles
High-heeled dung beetles
   Drive-by dreams
   Gentrified jungle gym schemes
Back-alley chants
Street corner rants
   Homeless pigeons
   Cacophonous religions
Scabby knees
Government surplus cheese
   Cardboard castles
   Welfare bureaucratic hassles
Trigger-happy hopes
Target practice floats
   Piss parades
   Miserable days
Fossil fuel emission haze
Asthmatic wheezing strays
   Broken fire escape dreams
   Bursting concrete seams
Hip hop harassments
Fashion plate enchantment
   Angry fat chochas
   Calculated faux pas
Masticating streets
Dog shit heaps
   Irate squirrels & hostile pigeons
   Black bean burrito fissions
Old folks mugging you with dentures
Homeless as statues & furniture
   Flying manhole covers
   Rats who hiss & hover
Museum mausoleums
Syringe serum
   Plexiglass graves
   Subway caves
Low-income cemeteries
Frustration factories
   Black smoke umbrellas
   Air-conditioned lovers

Nervous breakdown mothers
Belching cracked sewer covers
   Coughing clouds
   Lonesome crowds
Loathsome loaves of bread
The walking dead
   Display case rage
   Young old age
High school cages
Underground mazes
   Rust & ash
   Lust & rash
Holy communion hash
Phenolbarbital car crash
   Lower back tattoos & hair extensions glue
   Every half hour the rent is due
Lounge lizards & liquid lovers
Red track marks white garter belts & blue covers
   Slaphappy hooligans
   What's old is new again
Flat-footed fascists
Holy spoken word rhapsodists
   Canned cat food abductions
   Corrupt corruption
Unnecessary redundancy
Decadence & sleaze
   Sunshine & freeze
   Happy feet & broken knees
On the verge of a nervous break dance beat
Hovering heaping hip hop heat
   Corporate welfare cheats
   Tax evading feats
Homeless bourgeois winos
Media hacks & political ho's
   Poodles in three-piece suits
   Gold tooth jheri curl mannequins in Timberland boots
Prison pampered pimp strolling chumps
Apple Bottom humps
   Death as a Thanksgiving Day Parade float
   Evangelical rote

Popsicle stick boats
Glad Ziploc bag moats
   Rusted cars used as slop jars
   High society barroom brawls
Sleepwalking rotting meat
Belching street grater gutter heat
   Fifth floor walk-up ashtrays
   Alupent inhaler roach spray
Early morning brown yellow phlegm sleet
Cardboard sheets
   Marble flesh
   Agent orange stress
Pink slips & eviction whips
Maraca hips
   Geriatric gangbangers
   Aborted wire hangers
High fructose corn syrup fire hydrants
Occupied military migrants
   Plastic palm trees
   Psychedelic fleas
Government-sanctioned disease
Everybody say, *Surplus cheese!*

I want to stick my head
   In a latrine of lies

   I want to roll around
In a blanket full of hives

I want to wrap myself
   In a patchwork quilt of hunger cries

   I want to shower
In a hail of bombs that swarm like flies

Ever love a woman
   You love her too damn much
Ever love a woman so mean
   You gives her flowers, candies and such and such
She pay you back with a switchblade to your gut

I know it might sound violent
   It might sound extreme
But did you ever loves a woman oh so mean
   Breath carnation milk sweet
But what come out her nostrils is steam

Ever love a woman
   Who flips just like a switch
One minute she's battin' her lashes smilin'
   The next minute she got you
Lyin' in a ditch

I got an on-and-off woman
   Who loves me on and off
One minute she says I love you
   The next minute she scowls
And scoffs

For my birthday she gave me
   A bottle of my favorite gin
Said she gave me a big ol'
   Bottle of sweet
Down home sinnin' gin

Heavy as lead
   Then got to drinkin'
And thinkin'
   And blinkin'
And bashed it over my head

Went to the doctor
   To work on her head
Went to the doctor
   To fix what's broke in her head
Ol' Doc ended up mendin' mine instead

Indignant Blues

I poured twenty-nine years
Of my life into a no-good dirty job
I poured all my energy and time
Into this ragtag job

Only for my boss to tell me
Watch out for the doorknob
Like he was doin' me a favor
Like pimp smacked bottom lip blood
Was my favorite flavor

I was a few cranks-on-the-clock
From retirin' and gettin' my pension
I was oh so close to retirin'
And gettin' away with my pension

When they laid me off without no warning
Tellin' me I wouldn't have no job
And no pension in the mornin'

I said you gots to be kiddin' me
And kiss my ass
You heard me right
I said you outta yo got damn mind
And kiss my big ol' rusty ass

Tellin' me I ain't got a job
While sittin' with your feet all propped up
As matter of factly as you yawnin'

Pink Slip Blues

Some times are worse than others
And for others times are worse
When life don't treat you proper
And you don't understand your worth

Pink used to be my favorite color
Until my boss gave me the slip
Pink used to drive me crazy
Until the boss man made it unhip

Life is like a barge
And you ain't on that ship
When pink is your color
And your boss gives you the slip

Occupy Some Clean-Ass Drawers
    Occupy Lockjaw
Occupy a Lie
    Occupy a Sty in the Eye
Occupy Common Sense
    Occupy a Borderless Fence
Occupy Reality
    Occupy TV
Occupy Some Fishnet
    Occupy Free Rent
Occupy a Concept
    Occupy No Debt
Occupy Your Mama's Arms
    Occupy No Arms
Occupy Peace Instead of War
    Occupy Charm & a Banana Peel
Occupy Roosevelt's New Deal
    Occupy a Baby's Smile
Occupy the Here & Now
    Occupy Hazmat Boots
Occupy Big Bank Loot
    Occupy Toxic Sludge Lungs
Occupy a Broke Ladder's Rungs
    Occupy The White House
Occupy Mickey Mouse
    Occupy a Ham Sandwich
Occupy a Six-Foot Ditch
    Occupy a Melting Clock
Occupy a Blanket of Chickenpox
    Occupy a Bay of Pigs
Occupy a Bundle of Twigs
    Occupy Algae Slime
Occupy a Vowel-Less Rhyme
    Occupy a Hole in the Head
Occupy Red Riding Hood's Grandmama's Bed
    Occupy the Sands of Time
Occupy White-Collar Crime
    Occupy Emotional Embezzlement
Occupy Resentment

Occupy Graffiti Excrement
Occupy Shoes Made Out of Cement
Occupy a Splinter in Your Ass
Occupy Glaucoma Grass
Occupy Diamonds in the Sky
Occupy a Far Out High
Occupy the Moon & the Stars
Occupy a Porn Star's Scars
Occupy Sagging Tit Tattoos
Occupy the Broke Dick Dog Blues
Occupy an Irate Iambic Pentameter
Occupy a Ball Peen Hammer
Occupy a Chalupa Bean Burrito & Tacos
Occupy a Lowrider Car Full of Vatos
Occupy the Madness of Muscatel
Occupy Dante's Third Circle of Hell
Occupy a Couch Potato Beer Fart
Occupy Conceptual Art
Occupy the Eye of the Storm
Occupy What's Not the Norm
Occupy the Glove Compartments of the Rich
Occupy the Stink but Not the Itch
Occupy the Clenched Teeth of a Tase
Occupy the Policeman's Baton Whack Daze
Occupy the Spoken Word
Occupy a Dodo Bird
Occupy Frida Kahlo's Brow
Occupy the Jones without the Dow
Occupy a Sticky Chewed-Up Now & Later
Occupy the Clamp of an Alligator
Occupy the Kingdom of Heaven
Occupy a 7-11
Occupy a Sack of Schweddy Balls
Occupy Buster Keaton Slapstick Pratfalls
Occupy Your Hand in Mine
Occupy a Flowerpot Bustelo Can
Occupy a Grain of Sand
Occupy Fake Wars for Overflowing Oil Wells
Occupy Federal Prison Cells

Occupy a Port-O-John
     Occupy a Donkey Kong Bong
Occupy a Literary Allusion
     Occupy Corporate-State Collusion
Occupy the Myth of Menstruation Sin
     Occupy a Carved-Out Bible with a Bottle of Gin
Occupy a Snowflake on Your Tongue
     Occupy a Song That Is Sung
Occupy a Bleeding Heart on a White Ruffled Sleeve
     Occupy the Tears of a Child in Need
Occupy the Ism of the Schism
     Occupy Every Spectrum of a Prism
Occupy Every Hue in a Man
     Occupy All That You Can
Occupy Each Blade of Grass Springing from Each Pore
     Occupy the Crack the Leak & the Open Door
Occupy the Beat the Bass the Hum & the Drum
     Occupy the Wall the Street & the New Day to Come

Something Hip Hop This Way Comes

*Sometimes with the beats
comes a beating*

BLING BLING

These days

    The shackles

        Are shinier

HIP HOP HURTS SOMETIMES

Sometimes with the beats comes a beating.

She was caught by surprise
        Two words
Raised up against her
        Like fists
The bling of brass knuckles
        Disguised as gold teeth
Crashing down on her
        From the booming
Speakers in the trunk
        Of an SUV
Hip Hop hurts sometimes
        These words said
Riding on the backend
        Of an unavoidable beat
Like the backhand
        Of a pimp
Like the catcalls
        Of old cats
Holding up the corner
        With forties and blunts
All she wanted to do
        Was go to the corner store
And get some Pampers
        For her little sister
Get some Wonder Bread
        And Now and Laters
Get a Diet Pepsi
        And a 7Up
For her grandmother
        And aunt
But these words
        Made it hard for her
They knocked her
        Upside her head
Like her stepfather
        Trying to snatch
Her innocence
        Like her jealous boyfriend
Trying to control her life

Wasn't the usual
Yo, Shorty
       Let me get those digits
I'm a producer
       Or the slow crawl
Of cars creeping
       Along the curb
Trying to get her attention
       But something heavy
With a boxer's bass
       Something hard and smacking
Like a Barry Bonds blast
       Knocked her
Upside her head
       So hard
Her ego shrank
       Her self-esteem
Cowered in the corner
       Of her mind
Made her dizzy
       Made her confused
She was disoriented
       And delirious
Could hardly make it up the stairs
       The ringing would not stop
Reverberated like a
       Break dance beat
Breaking inside her head
       She wondered if it
Was true
       What she heard
What stuck to her
       Like dog shit
On the bottom of her shoe
       Was true
At thirteen what did she know
       Was she actually
A bitch
       And a ho

Was that what
      Her brother thought
Was that what
      Her father thought
Is that what her uncles
      And cousins
And all men think
      Those two words
Made their way through
      The irresistible beat
Made their way through
      The overwhelming heat
Of that hot summer street
      Climbed up out
Of the speakers
      Bumrushing her
Catching her by surprise
      Lies darting about
Like a prizefighter's
      Lightning fast gloves
Snatching something from her
      The flash and bling of brass knuckles
Giving her a shiner
      A blue black reminder
Dubious stars twirling like flies
      Just above her head
She felt nauseous
      Dropped her bags
Clutching her flat stomach
      Bent over in the staircase
Crying uncontrollably
      Tears huge and heavy
And hot with hurt
      Each drop a branding iron stain of pain
Poured out of her
      Like buckets of blood
As if she were pregnant
      With something dead

BLUE SCOWL AUBADE

She wore a scowl on her face like foundation & mascara
    Smearing into ruby red lips the color of Dorothy's slippers
        Gone to take her home with a click—only her lips

Repelled ghosts with their bent twisted handlebar mustache
    Frown like a clown down on his luck—buried beneath bills &
        Faded thrills—beneath pink slips & slipped banana peel

Back flips of Vicodin sin & gin—not the proper tonic but a
    Buzz that'll do—to beat back the flies with dry harsh
        Howling breath even the wind despised

Disguised in grief, in a blues so old & familiar
    She walked the streets in
        Cold stares swirling from lampposts & pavements

Speckled with dirty gum & broke glass shards
    Twinkly-eyed as if the cement drank rum
        She found it hard to get high

The numb feeling receding like a ship
    From her foolish shore
        Love done gone & split done packed its bags

Like a guitar in the hands of a blues man
    Rolling out of town on a midnight freight
        Hauling him off like a bucket full of pain

Wrapped in Ziploc bags— all she ever had—
    Her life carted from corner to
        Corner rattling around on squeaky wheel heels

What she concealed in the coat someone left
    Draped over her like a quilt or cape she could not
        Escape beneath an uptown el as she slumbered

Restlessly on cardboard splayed out on concrete &
    Cold—her world reduced to oil stains & piss
        Smells some wino left trying to drown out an ant's dawn song

Clumps of newsprint torn out black-and-white photos
    The yellowed pages of outdated copy stuffed her like a
        Turkey to keep her warm and basting for the taking

The plucking of dirty pigeons that shat on her sleeping
    Statue of flesh torn out holes in pants & shoes
        Howling at indiscriminate rats rolling like

Gangbangers who just don't give a fuck gonna
    Get what's theirs, mad 'hood—like all the
        Men in her life—taking what they could

AQUA SOLO
for Albert Ayler

Blue heart stopped like broke down bus
That last dime slipped from pocket lint
Caught in street crack like trapped fly
Blue tear hangs on clef note chin
Pillow wet and warm with blue pain
Window clouded with yellow tulips' mustard wounds
Blue death crawls from sax man's tomb

THINGS TO BLAME HIP HOP FOR

White Hate
Watergate

Exxon Valdez
Government Surplus Cheese

Three Mile Island Nuclear Haste
The Iraq War Waste

Black Genocide and White Cloning
Global Warming

AIDS
No Knock Raids

Unwanted Pregnancies
Corporate Hostilities

Skipping Out on the Check
The Titanic's Sinking Deck

Prison Work with No Check
The World Trade Center Wreck

Eddie Murphy in *Shrek*
WIC Checks

Classism Schism
Environmental Racism

The Spanish Inquisition
Driving with No Ignition

Sodom and Gomorrah
Cancer-Causing Cremora

Hurricane Katrina
Oscar Meyer's Weiner

The Tsunami
Police Brutality

The Middle Passage
The Coining of the Term Islamo Fascist

The Trail of Tears
Coors Beer

Nazi Germany
Black Poverty

*If it don't fit
You must acquit!*

Class Ten Caustic Poison
Jim Crow fire Hydrant Hosin'

Depleted Uranium
Meth Labs and Lithium

The Iran Contra Affair
Weapons of Mass Destruction Scare

Genocide in the Sudan
Mantan Moreland

Microwave Melted Tupperware
Christianized Permed Straightened Hair

The Price of Oil
Irradiated Soil

Hiroshima
Condoleezza

Privatized Prisons
Nuclear Fissions

The Good Ship Jesus
Butthead & Beavis

Mass Graves
Cotton Picking Days

US-Backed Guatemalan Death Squads
US-Instigated Islamic Jihads

The Medellin Cartel
The Marriage of Heaven & Hell

Japanese Internment Camps
Wall Street Tramps

Menstrual Cramps
Skin Shade Lamps

15-Minutes of Fame Vamps
Enron Scamps

Highway Projects Tank Off Ramps
Elvis Presley Postage Stamps

Afro Sheen
The Poetry in *The New Yorker* Magazine

Pork Chop Breath Preachers
History-Challenged Teachers

High Cholesterol Holy Rollers
Baby's Mama Broken Strollers

C. Delores Tucker CD Steamrollers
Gold-Capped Molars

Toilet Roll Hair Rollers
Welfare Cheese Dolers

Wha'sa matter boss, we sick?
Country Music

Whitney & Bobby
Cops Killing Black Men As a Hobby

The Homeless Sleeping in a Cardboard Box Lobby
The Ruphi Sex Allegations of Bill Cosby

Cyanide
DDT Pesticide

Agent Orange
Rwandan Carnage

Cambodian Killing Fields Slaughter
Jeb Bush's Coke-Sniffing Daughter

Atlantic Slave Trade Degradation
Crack As a Form of Reparation

Kramer vs. KKKramer
N-word Disclaimer

But here's the real scoop
I'm all that and then some,
I'm short dark and handsome
Bust a nut inside your eye,
To show you where I come from.

—A Tribe Called Quest

Things to Hang Don Imus On

Imus adopts a pair of African children
To cover his on-air racist rant(s)
But is seen wearing them like alligator shoes

Imus admits that Al Jolson is his favorite singer;
That he imitates him on his ranch when
He's alone with his sheep

Imus speaks in his sleep of fondness
For black shoe polish

Imus suspected of taking naps between
Vitriolic thoughts

Imus dribbles when he thinks

Imus bust a nut

Imus go

On Laura Schlessinger and Her N-Word Rant

I

If she would've
　　Said nigger
One more time
　　She would've had

An orgasm

It would've been
　　Her first
In 90 years—
　　The old battle axe

Her wrinkles would've
　　Bunched up in her
Throat like a
　　Gag order

II

nigger
　nigger
　nigger
nigger
　nigger
　　nigger
nigger
　nigger
nigger
　nigger
nigger

Dr. Laura Schlessinger rinsing her mouth in the morning.

Belt Buckle Nameplates of Presidential Candidates

Rosary Bling

Oprah Divas That Can't Sing

Salt & Vinegar Catholic Holy Communion Body of Christ Wafers

O.E. from a .40 for the Blood of Christ

Private Mister Softee Chasers

Prison-Style Pampers That Sag Off a Baby's Ass

Graffiti Wheaties

Wu Tang Clan McDonald's Hand Puppets

Hip Hop Grammar Books

Yo, What Up, Son Down with Jesus T-shirts

Closed Captions for the Hip Hop Impaired

Designer G-Strings

Gold-Plated Chicken Wings

Passive-Aggressive Hip Hop Hip Huggers

Keepin' It Real Pre-Apic Old School Can & String Cell Phones

Yo, Shorty, I'm a Producer, Let Me Get Those Digits Ring Tones

Pimp Posters

New & Improved In-Your-Face Pubic Hair-Laced DeBeers Diamond Encrusted Grills

Down Low Hip Hop Nom de Plumes Taken from Popular Cereal Brands
(Trix/Frosted Flakes/Fruit Loops/Raisin Bran)

Halloween Masks with Hip Hop Grimaces

Rap Lyrics Calling Pigeons & Squirrels Bitches & Ho's

Redneck Rap Videos with Sheep & Other Barnyard Animals in Thongs & G-Strings
(*Whoomp Dare It Iz!*)

Time-Saving *Nah Mean*? Conversation Flashcards

Flava Flav Black Velvet Portraits

Ol' Dirty Bastard Big Baby Jesus Dirt McGirt Welfare ID Card House Slippers

Biz Markie Contact Lenses

Nonchalant Club Casual Outings of Down Low Hip Hop Heads—*My man Fruity Pebbles is in the house!*

Shakespearean Shout-Outs in Irate Iambic Pentameter

Fashion Shows with Day-Glo Straitjackets, Orange Jumpsuits, Potato Sack Three-Piece Suits, High-Heeled Glass Slipper Timbs & Chain Gang Auction Block Ball & Chain Bling

P. Diddy Inspired Monosyllabic Vowel-Less Rhymes

EKG Machines with Hardcore Hip Hop Beats

Airbrushed Mug Shots

Spinning Tricycle Rims

Velvet Rope Crime Scene Tape

Graffiti Chalk-Marked Silhouettes

Pre-Recorded *I Wanna Thank Jesus* Acceptance Speeches for Rap Songs Stressing Animosity Towards Bitches, Ho's & Other Assorted Baby Mamas

Graffiti Greeting Cards

Ghetto Beatdown Singing Telegrams

Hip Hop Orthopedic Shoes

Rough Rider Porcupine Prophylactics

Keepin' It Real Method Acting Classes

THE KEEPIN' IT REAL AWARDS

Best Welfare Cheat

Best Empty Beer Can Collector

Best Ant & Roach Killer

Best Broke Back Mountain Rat Rider

Best Drive-By Shooting Victim

Best Crime Scene Tape Cordoner

Best Chalk-Marked Silhouette Model

Best Stripper in a Turquoise Thong

Best Toilet Roll Holder

Best Projects' Elevator Pisser

Best Jheri Curl Weave

Best Gold Toofus

Best Crack Attack Running Man Dancer Breaking & Scraping Along the Concrete Until Your Limbs Bleed

Best Sisyphean Government Surplus Cheese Hauler

Best Mister Softee Chaser

Best Popsicle Stick Race Along the Curbside Fire Hydrant Stream

Best Lower Back Tattoo

Best Dry Hump Beneath a Staircase

Best Heroin-Induced Vomit Nod

Best Hip Hop Grimace

Best Pallbearer

EVERYTHING YOU WANTED TO KNOW ABOUT HIP HOP BUT WERE AFRAID TO BE HIPPED FOR FEAR OF BEING HOPPED

Hip Hop Halitosis Hip Hop Hosiery Hip Hop Haberdashery Hip Hop Hollandaise Sauce Hip Hop Alupent Inhaler Hip Hop Hysterectomy Hip Hop Viagra Hip Hop Lamborghini Hip Hop Chanclettas Hip Hop Unemployment Hip Hop Fortune Cookie Hip Hop Auction Block Hip Hop Umbrella Hip Hop Rocking Chair Hip Hop Chandelier Hip Hop Hool-a-Hoop Hip Hop Hooray Hip Hop Hurricane Hip Hop Quagmire Hip Hop Radial Tire Hip Hop Earth Wind & Fire Hip Hop Muck & Mire Hip Hop Hotwire Hip Hop Perspire Hip Hop Fire & Desire Hip Hop Murder for Hire Hip Hop Liar Hip Hop Sire Hip Hop Retirement Plan Hip Hop & the Man Hip Hop Hooligan Hip Hop Bogeyman Hip Hop Sanitation Truck Hip Hop Don't Give a Fuck Hip Hop Can You Spare a Buck Hip Hop Desperation Hip Hop Inflation Hip Hop Hives Hip Hop Urtication Hip Hop Meditation Hip Hop Medication Hip Hop Tokyo Rose Hip Hop Potato Chips Hip Hop Stovetop Stuffing Hip Hop Putrefaction Hip Hop Pepto Bismal Hip Hop Pundit Hip Hop Fund It Hip Hop Brothel Hip Hop Silverware Hip Hop Crystal Stair Hip Hop Buyer Beware Hip Hop Nuclear Scare Hip Hop Dental Care Hip Hop Fred Astair Hip Hop Flair Hip Hop Nightmare Hip Hop Tupperware Hip Hop Hair Hip Hop Stare Hip Hop Chair Hip Hop Bear Hip Hop Share Hip Hop Glare Hip Hop Air Hip Hop Where Hip Hop Heir Hip Hop Dare Hip Hop Holocaust Hip Hop Hucklebuck Hip Hop Helium Hip Hop Delirium Hip Hop Landing Hip Hop Scanning Hip Hop Canning Hip Hop Fanning Hip Hop Tanning Salon Hip Hop Rayon Hip Hop Ding Dong Hip Hop Donkey Kong Hip Hop Churning Hip Hop Is Burning Hip Hop Earning Hip Hop Learning Hip Hop Discerning Hip Hop Ham Sandwich Hip Hop Pork Rinds Hip Hop Spare Ribs Hip Hop Ham on Rye Hip Hop Lady Di Hip Hop High Five Hip Hop Hard Drive Hip Hop Wanted Dead or Alive Hip Hop Beehive Hip Hop Jive Hip Hop Sour Cream and Chives Hip Hop Dives Hip Hop Wives Hip Hop Friendly Skies Hip Hop Handle Hip Hop Scandal Hip Hop Cross Your Heart Bra Hip Hop Crossword Puzzle Hip Hop Crossing Hip Hop Bossing Hip Hop Salad Tossing Hip Hop Dental Floss Hip Hop Hobby Horse Hip Hop Mister Ed Hip Hop Mr. Potato Head Hip Hop Freddy's Dead Hip Hop Pro Keds Hip Hop Giving Head Hip Hop Lead Hip Hop Better Dead Than Red Hip Hop Shed Hip Hop Dread Hip Hop Sled Hip Hop Feds Hip Hop Rorschach Test Hip Hop Rutabaga Hip Hop Scapular Hip Hop Spatula Hip Hop Ambiguity Hip Hop Anxiety Hip Hop Quadruped Hip Hop Acumen Hip Hop Chihuahua Hip Hop Stockpile Hip Hop Projectile Hip Hop Cake with File Hip Hop Gomer Pile Hip Hop Dream Weaver Hip Hop Dumb

Beaver Hip Hop Back Alley Hip Hop Rally Hip Hop White Trash Hip Hop
Monster Mash Hip Hop Moroccan Hash Hip Hop Pipes Hip Hop Swipes Hip
Hop Baby Wipes Hip Hop Snipes Hip Hop Gripes Hip Hop Stereotypes Hip
Hop Dukes of Hazard Hip Hop Ol' Dirty Bastards Hip Hop Hotel Hip Hop
Motel Hip Hop Holiday Inn Hip Hop Constipation Hip Hop Chia Pet Hip
Hop Seeing Eye Dog Hip Hop Kermit the Frog Hip Hop Closed Captions
Hip Hop Subtitles Hip Hop Country Club Hip Hop City Hip Hop Boo Boo
Kitty Hip Hop Itty Bitty Titty Committee Hip Hop Pity Hip Hop Diddy Hip
Hop Eponymy Hip Hop Economy Hip Hop Sunlight Hip Hop Ultra Bright
Hip Hop Out of Sight Hip Hop Fly by Night Hip Hop Fly a Kite Hip Hop
Despite Hip Hop Drawers Hip Hop Hog Maws Hip Hop Tattoo Paws Hip
Hop Broken Jaws Hip Hop Flaws Hip Hop Crawls Hip Hop Shores Hip
Hop Snores Hip Hop Bronchitis Hip Hop Meningitis Hip Hop Gold Tooth
Gingivitis Hip Hop Grammar Book Hip Hop Graham Crackers Hip Hop
Quarterback Sackers Hip Hop Weed Whackers Hip Hop Dunkin Donut
Snackers Hip Hop Crumb Snatchers Hip Hop Booty Smackers Hip Hop
Asthma Attack Hip Hop Comeback Hip Hop Hooligan Hip Hop Stool Pigeon
Hip Hop Incision Hip Hop Derision Hip Hop Precision Hip Hop Aneurysm
Hip Hop Harvey Wall Banger Hip Hop No More Wire Hangers Hip Hop
Apologia Hip Hop Mama Mia Hip Hop Candy Yams Hip Hop Credit Card
Scams Hip Hop Winnebago Hip Hop Let My People Go Hip Hop Let
Go My Eggo Hip Hop Shake 'N' Bake Hip Hop Frosted Flakes Hip Hop
Earthquakes Hip Hop On a Plane with Snakes Hip Hop These Are the Breaks
Hip Hop Fugazi Jewelry Fakes Hip Hop Wakes Hip Hop Makes Mistakes
Hip Hop Morphine Drip Hip Hop Liposuction Hip Hop Facelift Hip Hop
Temper Tantrum Hip Hop Prenup Hip Hop D-Up Hip Hop Layup Hip
Hop Layoff Hip Hop Pink Slip Hip Hop Sinking Ship Hip Hop Chocolate
Chip Hip Hop Dip Hip Hop Trip Hip Hop Sip Hip Hop Similac Hip Hop
Stevedore Hip Hop I Adore Hip Hop Mi Amor Hip Hop Fundamentalist
Hip Hop Insanity Hip Hop Payola Hip Hop Crayola Hip Hop Barbie Hip
Hop Stretch Marks Hip Hop Robitussin High Hip Hop Epidemic Hip Hop
Epidural Hip Hop Pandemic Hip Hop Pandora's Box Hip Hop Pancake
Mix Hip Hop Panic Button Hip Hop Pedantic Hip Hop Eye Tic Hip Hop
Puritanical Hip Hop Botanical Hip Hop Purist Hip Hop Fingerprints Hip Hop
Nation Hip Hop Escalation Hip Hop Exclamation Mark Hip Hop After Dark
Hip Hop Orthopedic Shoes Hip Hop Hebrews Hip Hop EKG Machine Hip
Hop Figurine Hip Hop Dis&Dat Hip Hop Hazmat Hip Hop Mummies Hip
Hop Crash Test Dummies Hip Hop Hydroplane Hip Hop Down the Drain

TWATTING AROUND ON TWITTER

I wake up.

I'm scratching my ass.

I take a big dump.

It's a steaming hot mess of hostility.

It's brutal.

Like sheep my bowels are bleating.

It takes me back to my Lincoln Logs childhood days.

There are Tonka trucks from the 1970s embedded somewhere in there.

I shave.

I'm taking a shower.

I hope this Crackberry doesn't short circuit or drown.

OMG, there's no hot water!

I nearly have a heart attack when the cold water shocks me out of my skin.

After I floss and shave and chafe my skin, I have a thought.

It is fleeting.

Somewhere a sheep is bleeding.

OMG, it's my ex's Maxi-Pad—

Emphasis on MAXI.

OMG, grosso!

On the windowsill bushy-browed bespectacled pigeons are eating

Stella Dora breadsticks like Groucho with a cigar.

On top of trees beneath my window squirrels are feeding

On nuts.

I'm glad they're not mine.

BESTSELLER, REQUIRED TEXT, THE FUTURE OF BLACK LITERATURE?

Super Ho by Quantilla Shabazz

When Chickenheads Come Home to Roast by Bookman Shame

Clementine Whore by Latanya Monet Prince

What Some Stank Bitch Want by LaPrincia Hortense Gallagher

Castrated Convict Cocks on Lock by Huey Pete

CLI-TOE-WRIS by D'Andre

Every Stank Ho Need Love Sometime by Keisha LaBlanc

Nigga Wha'? by Dingleberry Juice

Pants Off the Cliff of My Ass by D.J. McNutts

I Told the Bitch I Was Gay, So What If She Got AIDS by D.L. Anonymous

Thugella by Cynthia Spykes

Every Pimp Ain't No Preacher by Ice Pick English

Every Preacher Need a Hustle by Ice Pick English

Apollo G's on My Knees by Raspberry Bonnet

Ten Commandments of a Hustler by Moe Zus

Jailhouse ResErection by G. Zus

Whore You Kidding? by ChiChi ChaCha

Whore You Lookin' At? by ChiChi ChaCha

Blow Jobs from Brazil by Itchy Stink

Portobello Pork Chop Penis by Pablo Pissant

E. Litter Rah C. by Catty James

Shit Slam Squat & Pee Slam Bacon & Eggs Slam Ham on Rye Slam Shit
on Shinola Slam Spit & Drool Slam Vomit Slam Back Alley Wino Piss
Slam Maggots Crawling Out an Open Skull Slam Backstabbing Slam
Eviction Slam Ass on Pavement Slam Prescription Slam Hungry Man Slam
Starvation Slam Bombs Bursting in Air Slam Dead Roach in Spaghetti Slam
Dumb Motherfuckers Can't Think for Self Slam Reading is Detrimental
Slam Cain & Able Slam Gentrification Slam Globalization Slam Hull of a
Slave Ship Slam Middle Passage Slam Ku Klux Klan Slam Goosestep Heil
Hitler Nazi Slam Gas Chamber Slam Sodomy Slam Full Frontal Lobotomy
Slam One Flew Over the Cuckoo's Nest Slam I Don't Give a Damn Slam
Genocide Slam Smallpox in Blankets for Indians Slam Thanksgiving Day
Slam Resurrection Slam Dead Cock Forklift Viagra Slam Stank Ho Slam
Auction Block Slam Kill Whitey Slam Maroon Slam Macheteros Slam
Boukman Slam Toussaint L'Ouveture Slam Jean Jacques Dessalines Slam
Che Slam Fidel Slam Nat Turner Slam John Brown Slam Sandinista Slam
Al-Qaeda Slam Weapons of Mass Destruction Slam HIV Slam AIDS Slam
Anthrax Slam Ebola Soup Slam UN Troops Slam Avian Flu Slam Agent
Orange Slam Muscatel Slam Mad Dog Slam Ripple Slam Gut Bucket
Blues Slam Rot Gut Slam Cocaine Slam Crack Slam Crystal Meth Slam
Preemptive Slam Slam National Security Slam Defense Department
Manufacture AIDS Slam Bush Administration Bomb the World Trade
Center & the Pentagon to Go to War with the Middle East & Snatch Up
Oil Wells & Undermine the Euro Slam Your Mother's a Two-Face Slam
Poppa Was a Rolling Stone Slam 40 Acres & a Mule Slam Reparations
Slam Zionism Slam Gaza Strip Slam Infitada Slam Suicide Bomber Slam
Stolen Land Slam Son of Sam Slam I Am What I Yam Slam Green Eggs &
Ham Slam High Blood Pressure Slam Sugar Slam Booger Slam Bling Bling
Slam Sing Sing Slam Sick & Demented Slam Jimmy Superfly Snucka Slam
Spanish Fly Slam Spanish Inquisition Slam Conquistador Slam Christopher
Columbus Slam Cuttie Sark Slam Buffalo Soldier Slam Dreadlock Rasta
Slam Philistine Slam Afro Sheen Slam Colgate & Listerine Slam Robin
Island Slam Apartheid Slam Free Winnie Mandela Slam Negroes with
Guns Slam Pedophile Priests & Mean Nuns with Big Rulers Slam James
Brown Don't Want None Won't Be None Slam We Bombed in Baghdad
Slam Iraq Cradle of Civilization Reduced to Barney & Betty Rubble Slam
Israelis Genociding Palestinians Slam Scentless Bombs Slam Wailing Wall
Slam Tears for Fears Slam Blood for Oil Slam Human Cargo Slam NY
Life Slave Insurance Slam Trans Atlantic Slave Trade Globalization Slam

Goree Island Slam Elmira Slave Castle Slam Exxon Mobile Slam Watergate
Slam Iran Contra Slam Guatemalan Genocide Slam Forced Migration Slam
Media Manipulation Slam Embedded Journalists Slam Church & State
Slam State & Corporate Slam Eleanor Bumpers Slam Underdevelopment
Slam Internment Camp Slam Concentration Camp Slam Reservation Blues
Slam Whites Only Slam COINTELPRO Slam FBI Slam CIA Slam Tonton
Macoute Slam Das Boot Slam Il Duce Slam Antonio Gramsci Slam Skull
& Crossbones Illuminati Slam Kiss My Black Ass Slam Bitch Better Have
My Money Slam Punks Jump Up to Get Beat Down Slam Capitalism &
Christianity Slam The Marriage of Heaven & Hell Slam Abu Grab Slam
Torture Slam Right-Wing Reactionary Sociopath Slam Population Control
Slam War Crimes Slam I Ain't Gonna Study War No More Slam O Slam
My Best Friend Gayle Slam Stedman & I Slam O Sam I Am Slam Spam
Slam Astispumante Slam Hey, You Got Your Chocolate in My Peanut
Butter Broke Back Mountain Slam Sperm Juleps Slam Chunky Phlegm
Slam Taxation without Representation Slam Santería Slam Shangó Elégba
Slam Crayola Slam Payola Slam The Grassy Knoll Slam The Blown Out
Skull of Jack Kennedy Slam Ethnic Cleansing Slam Police Brutality Slam
All-White Juries Exonerating White Cops Slam Coup d'état Slam Regime
Change Slam Bitter Fruit Slam Black Reconstruction Slam Bay of Pigs
Slam Anti-American Activities Slam Collateral Damage Slam Electric
Chair Slam Shock & Awe Slam Scar Tissue Slam Eczema Slam INS Slam
Accelerated Sharing Slam World Bank Slam IMF Slam Another World
Is Possible Slam Planetary Protest Against War Slam DeBeers Diamond
Miners Slam A Piece of the Action Slam Petit Bourgeois Slam Genetic
Engineering Slam Petro Dollars Slam Idi Amin Dada Slam Mobutu Slam
Shanty Town Slam The G-8 Slam Riot Gear Slam Privatization Slam
Neo-Con Slam Neo-Liberalism Slam Driving Down Wages Slam Tax
Write-Off for Corporations Slam Good Governance Slam Obey the IMF
Slam Sweatshop Slam Say Hello to My Little Friend Slam Carpet Bagging
Slam Carpet Bombing Slam Carpet Cleaning Slam Carpet Cutting Slam
Carpet Burns Slam Carpet Munching Slam Carpe Diem Slam Corporate
Takeover Slam Corpus Christi Slam Carpal Tunnel Slam Constitutions That
Stipulate Only Whites Are Human Beings Slam WTO Slam Extra Virgin
Olive Oil Slam Sugarless Slam Fat-Free Slam Anorexic Slam Bulimic Slam
Regurgitation Slam Vomiting on the Side of a Ship Slam Tedious Extended
Metaphor Slam Everything in This Motherfucker but the Kitchen Sink Slam
The Kitchen Sink Slam

UPCOMING REALITY SHOWS

Dancing with the Homeless

Proctologists' Wives

Gynecologists in the Flesh

America's Next Top Bottom

Phlegm Nation

The Smegma Files

Kicking the Shit Out of the Kardashians

Paris Hilton Unplugged

Beyonce, Beyonce & More Beyonce:
*   Eating Popeye's Chicken, Giving Birth, Cutting an Album*
*   & Starring in Three Videos while Airbrushing Herself onto*
*   Fifty-two Magazine Covers All in the Same Day*

The Kanye Awards: Starring Just Kanye

BOOKS I NEED TO WRITE

Bum Stank the Ho

Bum Rush the Couch

*Penis Envy—When You Don't Get Along with Your Cock: A Midlife Crisis
Nightmare*

Christianity's the Reason Why You Perm Your Hair

Weave My Hair Alone

Pork 'N' Da Hood

Phlegm for Beginners

Sperm Juleps in Sodom

Viagra for Beginners

Prostate Pals

*Jew Keep Fuckin' Wit' Me and See What I'll Do: A Puerto Rican's Memoir
on What It's Like to Be Constantly Mistaken for a Palestinian*

Homeless in a McMansion

How to Stink and Not Itch

Spicanthropus Erectus

O My Colon is Powelless

Spanking Condi Rice

Justice Clarence Thomas: The Negro Years

*Conversations with Neo-Conservatives from the Shit-Stained Lips of a
Crumbling Commode*

*The Satanic Verses: Outtakes from George W. Bush's Favorite Quips &
Speeches*

Someday We'll All Be Fat-Free

Serious Trouble Will Bypass You

The Grim Reaper won't try to wake you up to make sure you're dead

SISYPHUS SPEAKS

for amiri b @ 70

Your hair could go white
As mine you roll a boulder

Uphill as many times I have
In my life

Hair can go white
Curse enough ghosts as I have

Hair whiter than John Brown's bones

ATLAS SHRUGGED

Confetti flesh tossed
Between the teeth of rain

    Predatory wind
    Blue wail
        Climbing out
A horn

    Like the sun
Singular bluebopcity
        Synchronized

Under the Manhattan Bridge
        Wind & rain
      More powerful than
          Sunlight & cranes
Rip your world
Like Atlas shrugged

          Steel & bone
          Flesh & soul

We are drinking
    Our wine
        In the café
           Window
As blood
Pours
    From the sky
    Glued to
Our seats
        To a world
Turned upside
    Down

These hairy shins
    Will go good
With asparagus tips

    A blind man
        Is dragging
        His dog
By the nose
          Bleeding

We are drinking
   Our wine
   In the café
Window
   Everyone
   Is cramming
To get
In

   The belly
Of the sax
   Is the hull
      Of a human cargo ship
     W a i l i n g

Pain never
Sounded so good

At the bottom
     Of the sea
   Be these bones
Beating

   What are
We
     Eating

One by one
The homeless
   Press their
Noses
     Against
     The pane

We ignore
Them
     Like flies

Is that a merlot
Or a sauvignon?

The forensics report
Contained a scratch & sniff
Snapshot, circa 1970s,
Close-up of a bullet hole
To the back of his head

The powder burns read:
He can't save money
He can't save his life
He can't save postage stamps
He can't save whales
Tonight

This was all recorded
Meticulously
Like a song

In not just
Any old register

Although the
Cha-ching cha-ching
Cha-ching
Was like a zing
Went the strings

Of my heart
Any romantic gesture
After this would be
Purely accidental

Speculative perhaps
Each slat
Removed from
The torso

To let light in
Would have to be removed
 Of cobwebs & dust

It's hard
Enough
For a black man

To hail a cab
In America
   Would be
   The anthem
But these
Tire marks
On the back
Of his head
   Tread lightly

    Here lies a
Mug shot   &
Blonde bobblehead
Here lies a money
Shot
To the porn star's head
A golf club, perhaps
Buried in the skull's
hole in one   O holy lowly one

   He wasn't
Hailing a cab
He was a bagger
A backwoods river dragger
Blasian ragin' blazin'
A trail—white wolves
on his tail

   He was amazin' a metaphor
     He was (ad)
Vance
   He was
     Similar
He was a simile
     For golf   in da club/at da house/da crib

He wasn't
Hailing a cab
   He was the driver

Sun & moon
Flies in June
  Death & taxes
Get the axes
  Political access
Of evil axis
  Wives & exes
Costly excess
  Romancing stones
Heroin love jones
  Skull & crossbones
Cyanide ice cream cones
  Sphincter moans
Early morning groans
  These old bones
Glass & splinter scones
  Getting beneath the skin
Of flesh & sin
  Till death do us part
Deception as art
  Perceptive depart
Perspective chart
  Body parts
Walmart
  Couch potato TV beer farts
Jalapeño black bean burritos
  Guacamole Cheetos
Molé with Fritos
  Supine & spread eagle
On a thin blue line
  Phenolbarbital & red wine
It pays to be kind
  To have a good mind
Bargain basement find
  Bottom feeders

In the pecking order
    Of prefabricated dreams
Get rich schemes
    Useless as spleens
& Afro Sheen
    On white girls who mean
No harm
    Hip & calm
Hysterical alarm
    Buy the farm
Frankly Scarlet
    I don't give a darn
Who your papa be
    C'est la vie
I gots my degree
    Oui Oui, Gigi
You won't be seein' me
    My chérie
Amour
    Labrador
Yeah right
    I'll retrieve ya
See ya
    Wouldn't wanna be ya
Paranoid & prissy
    High maintenance
& pissy
    Drunk & dizzy
Dazed & confused
    Angry & silly
Miss, your demeanor
    Gets meaner
With time
    Is it a crime
That I still love you

Cupid's arrow the size of a '74 Buick
Or a giant unripe squash from Woody Allen's
Sleeper caught hold of him in the PX at
Fort Gordon, Georgia, straight out of basic.
Love ran him down like the Tasmanian Devil
Rearranging his life like cheap Walmart furniture
That time he spotted her with Army fatigues &
Burgundy hair, searching for a discount box of Tampax.
Love left him baffled in a cloud of dust with
Tread marks on his back as if he were caught in the
Crossfire of a Road Runner-Wile E. Coyote chase scene.
Love insinuated itself into the folds of his frontal lobe
With all the subtlety of a TNT blast, an anvil
Dropped from a skyscraper of surprise—her aunt
Warned her on her wedding day, telling her, *He's a*
Pretty boy, you'll have to beat the women off with a stick—
Love dragged him kicking & screaming
Down the aisle of no return as if condemned to
A Mutiny on the Bounty short plank into the
Sea of what love used to be before the drowning,
Like the petrified, bloated flailing of a heart
Attack victim in the frozen foods section of
Pathmark, flopping about in epileptic desperation.
He never knew what hit him, he never knew what
Bit him, the day he slipped the ring on—amid
Hysterical pleas from his family & hers, *You're too*
Young! What is that your first piece?—
As his bride turned from Dr. Jekyll to
Mr. Hyde in one fell swoop that time at the
Dollar theater at the Viscount Blvd shopping mall
In the middle of the freight elevator scene
In *Fatal Attraction* when his wife turned
To him, her neck craning to the left in
Slow motion like Linda Blair in *The Exorcist*,
Anger & bitterness seething through the slits
Of her eyes at the standing heated exchange
Of on-screen lust & betrayal, to say—

                              All men are alike!

WHEN I THINK OF YOU, LOVE

I think of crop whips
Jackboots
Bile green berets
Cockeyed Cross Your Heart Bras
Black Marias &
Bomb-sniffing dogs

I think of the kindness
Of strangers
Red army ants
Cream of Wheat
Laced with cyanide
A bullet in the chamber
Rose petals pouting
On the windowsill
Prune juice &
Cold plump plums

When I think of you, Love
My feet get warm
Like Joan of Arc's
My heart pitter-patters
On the dining room floor
I get lockjaw
Chomping on the rare
Black Angus beef
You tenderized
With a ball peen hammer
& broken glass

I get gas
At the thought
Of you curdling
My milk
Like you curled
My toes—
One yank at a time,
The pliers proved too slick
To slip the proper grip,
Thank god thank god

When I think of you
I dribble & drool
I babble by the brook
The backyard turned into
After you evicted the Roto Rooter Man
With a lead pipe & two sticks
Of dynamite

When I think of you, Love
I remember how you tried
To convince me that
Cayenne pepper was
Paprika
& those Ginsu knives
You hurled my way,
Skinning my scalp
& nailing my collar
To the fridge,
Were car keys—
Baby please—
You could've
Handed them
To me

When I think of you, Love
I think of the Spanish Inquisition
Taxation without representation
Blankets stuffed with smallpox
I think of the Hindenburg
Hitler with Charlie Chaplin's mustache
A glow-in-the-dark rash
Water that's yellow
Phlegm-like Jello

I think of hell not having no fury
I think of a trial without a jury
I think of death camps
Advertised as resort hotels

I think of the Berlin Wall
Falling down on my head
& the subsequent
Price of bread
I think of Al Green hot grits to the nuts
I think of *Night of the Living Dead*
The living dead

SERIOUS TROUBLE WILL BYPASS YOU

(from a fortune cookie)

Serious trouble will bypass you
A safe will not fall on your head
A Roadrunner-Wile E. Coyote anvil will not crush every bone in your foot
You will not be riddled in a drive-by
Take up residence on a front lawn as a blood-spouting sprinkler
A roadside bomb will not make a smoky potpourri of your charbroiled flesh
Your heart will not collapse at the sight of pork chops
The IRS will not take away your kneecaps and have you sleeping with the
    fishes or cut your throat or get clobbered over the head at a Greek wedding
    from the exuberant tossing of dishes
You will not be evicted like dead fish tossed out onto a block of ice
The CIA will not inject you with a deadly flu
Your doctor will not drop a license plate in your open chest during surgery
The nursing home staff will not lace your diapers with itching powder and
    Krazy Glue
A Mack truck will not mow you down in the middle of the road
You will not be strangled by your airbag after being blindsided by a cross-
    town bus
A meteorite will not leave skid marks on the back of your head
The Grim Reaper won't try to wake you up to make sure you're dead
Your wife won't try to feed you a meatloaf seasoned with Class Ten caustic poison
You won't bite into a fast food burger stuffed with razors
The hormones from the chicken won't choke your chicken
You will not eat yourself out of house and home,
Roam the streets like an outpatient on Marzipan and Methadone
You won't choke on the remote and suffocate on a barrage of beer farts on
    your couch in a convulsive state of epileptic leisure
You will not be overcome with the sudden urge to jump off the side of a ship,
    stick your head in an oven or masturbate to death in 4-4 time
A gaggle of nuns will not beat you with rulers
A cacophony of phantom slave ship gas chamber killing field moans will not
    shrink wrap your ego into a parlor piece of paranoia atop a mantelpiece of
    indifference
You will not lose your mind in a bargain basement bin department store line
You will not be forced to prefabricate your dreams and order them over the
    phone like pizza
Your online date will not turn out to be a seriously ill cereal eating serial killer
    whose name is Captain Crunch and whose favorite line is *You're Great!*
    while turning your flesh and bones into Lucky Charms

You will not be smote by the hand of God—or two or three space aliens looking for Detroit

You will not be hogtied by a wet nurse with a fetish for Dominoes garlic knots dipped in prune juice marinara

You will not be violated with onion spears and asparagus tips

You will not be forced to name your firstborn daughter Chinchilla the Hun

You will not be forced to surrender your jazz CDs to right-wing fusionists trying to make a fascist statement

You will not be forced to consider the intellectual merits and social-political implications of Reality TV

You will not be forced to convert to the hip hop edition of the King James Bible

The radioactive waves from your cell phone will not reach into your ears and crush your brain like a grape

The rash on your ass will not be connected like dots by a tattoo artist with a blue period cubist fetish from Tijuana named Pablo Picante

The red white and blue flags up your ass will not be waved at half-staff

Some bored maniacal angst-ridden youth will not hack into your iPod and program it full of Lawrence Welk, Barry Manilow and country music

Warmongering oil barons will not invade your hair

Thugs will not give you hugs

Your children will not grow up to address you with: *What up, son?*

The overly-handled overly-indulged spoiled brats you raised with soccer TV videogames cell phones iPods laptops and shopping mall playgrounds will not end up saying, *Fuck you, Mom!,* every day except for a few hours on Mother's Day

Evidence-planting killer cops will not make a bouquet of guns out of your bashed-in skull

You will not be buried alive in a mulch pit peppered with the cannibalistic feces of barnyard animals

Your Viagra will not get mixed up with your high blood pressure pills

Your life won't end up a tragic comic punch line in a Greek chorus

Your wings won't get melted by the sun

You won't kill your father and sleep with your mother

You won't be forced to push a boulder up a hill

You won't be pushed off a windowsill

The Dow Jones Industrial Average will not push you off The Empire State Building

A gang of young street toughs will not douse you with lighter fluid and set you on fire as you sleep on a park bench

The Ozone Layer will not fall from the sky and smash you like a bug
You will not be torched like an ant under a magnifying glass by an
     unrelenting global warming sun
A tsunami will not leap up at you out of your backed-up kitchen sink as if it
     were a whale swallowing your Jonah
Irradiated water will not invade your bloodstream
A government-sanctioned deadly virus will not colonize your lungs
Your DNA will not be cleansed with Clorox or Listerine
You will not get Alzheimer's from jheri curl juice or Afro Sheen
Camel riding soldiers will not try to annihilate your genetic line
You will not be turned into a jigsaw puzzle of your former self
The cardboard box you live in will not be snatched up by a violent breeze
You will not be forced to drink bottle-cap wine
Beefy high fructose corn syrup stuffed kids will not try to turn your back into
     a hobbyhorse ride while you sleep on the curbside
Acid rain will not pockmark your hide
Your flesh will not be grinded into a spirited paté
Your body will not be turned into a communion wafer to appease the appetites
     and boredom of the bourgeoisie
Pseudo intellectual political hacks dressed in high priest gear will not accuse
     you of being a liar
You will not be forced to carry the wooden cross you'll be nailed to while
     wearing a makeshift crown made of concertina wire

Prices are sky high
Shrapnel falls in your eye

The cost of air does not plunge
Price tags scar your lungs

Wars are fought over water
Homeless the new human slaughter

Human flesh fed to dogs
Dogs dine on the legs of frogs

The latest fetish of the filthy rich
Who know how to stink and not itch

You'll find old ladies' trampled chins
At the bottom of bargain basement bins

Crushed in Black Friday adventures
Trying to retrieve their dentures

Rifling for canned cat food sales
For dinner to keep the wind's wails

From whistling through ribcage slats
Pieced together by dust and cobweb mats

Breadlines longer than canyon stretch marks
Starvation and stabbings the latest theme parks

Charcoal broiled air crowded with bombs
Clustered with cacophonous fire alarms

Like babies endless hysterical screaming
Each tree a bouquet of flames gleaming

COAL MINER'S SLAUGHTER

(Hymn from the International Coal Group Choir)

We don't mine and you don't matter
Just do your job and make us fatter
If you blow get trapped and die
We'll bury you like a soldier by and by

If you get black lung disease and cough and sneeze
Mine your manners don't fuss or show displease
Just pray to your Jesus quick heaven's return
Gotta move your carcass got coal to burn

Water supplies contaminated by spills
Air dusted with all that is ill
There is a chill a chill rolling off
Blue grass mountains that surround your
Trailers and seep through your pores

We ride on your back while you're
Down on all fours
We don't mine and you don't matter
Just do your job and make us fatter

You die in the mines while we laugh
To the bank
Life for you lived in a gas tank
That can blow at any moment

But you should give thanks
That you have a job that you have a job
Working for us

So don't fret or fuss when the mine goes bust
When your loved ones swallow ashes and dust

Life is not promised to those without wealth
We determine who gets sick who kicks and
Who's got health

'Cause we don't mine and you don't matter
'Cause you do the job that makes us fatter

CANNIBALS ON U STREET

for The Young Lions at Café Nema

Regardless of which nightstick
Hits you upside your head
It still cracks in 4-4 time

The streets still flow red
The gutter chokes on cherry blossoms
Rain splinters into kisses

Horses gallop out of horns
Punching holes through
Smoky neon air

Death is a woman
You mistook for a bass
Stringing her along

Somewhere a bomb is dropping
Somewhere a baby is screaming
Somewhere your mama is dreaming

You'll come home
You'll come home

QUESTIONS ON THE
POLICE OFFICER'S EXAM

In memory of Sean Bell (23), gunned down by the NYPD on his wedding day

How many bullets does it take to kill an unarmed black man?

Is excessive force an oxymoron?

Do you know what oxymoron means?

Do you know what an ox is?

Are you a moron?

What's worse driving under the influence or driving while black?

Are black men human?

If not, is Put-Your-Hands-on-the-Hood-of-the-Car a black man's
  nomenclature?

If a black man is felled in a forest and nobody hears it is it necessary to plant
  a gun in his open skull?

How *many* bullets does it take?

How many hits with a baton when hogtied?

How many whacks to the face?

How much blood is a disgrace?

How many tasers?

How much mace?

If he can't breathe does that leave a bad taste?

If he resists death is that a waste?

Is breathing considered resisting arrest?

Does a bullet in the back make the case?

Are handcuffs really necessary when faced down in an open grave?

BYRD ON A WIRE

In memory of James Byrd Jr., dragged to death behind a pickup truck
by three white supremacists in Jasper, Texas, on June 7, 1998

My head
   Rolls
      Away
         From me

In the street
   My eye
      Wonders why
         My body

Trembles into
   Itself
      How it
         Doesn't

Wave good
   Bye
      Following
         Behind

A pickup
   Truck
      Like a lazy
         Old rag doll

One arm
   Doesn't have
      The patience
         To stay

My legs
   Paint
      The town
         Red

Shangó's raging mouth
    Welt marks shining

In slavering sun
    Pomegranate surprise

Granddaddy's eyes
    Bulging above

A twisting
    Noose

Langston's Sue
    Sassin' along

Harlem street
    Malcolm big & bad

Straight from Detroit
    Shiny conk & crooked smile

On 125th & Lenox
    Getting his shoes shined

By my old man
    Trackmarks on his

Hands &
    His jones

Comin' down
    Comin' down

Coltrane's burning horn
    Cursing white men

Like tongue lash
    Of flame

Coursing through
    An Alabama church

DERRION SPEAKS FROM BLOOD ON CONCRETE

In memory of Derrion Albert (16), a Chicago Fenger H.S. honors student,
senselessly killed by other Black teens

Hey man, that's my boy
    You swinging at, my brother.
Grew up together—

Go to the same school.
    Those are his books turning red:
My blood on each page.

What was that you said?
    Don't give a damn 'bout books;
Rather bash brains in?

That's my DNA
    On your black skin red as sin—
Don't you know we kin?

I'm just askin', bruh—
    Watchu see in the mirror—
Hope's bloodstained scissors?

ALAS POOR RICHARD,
NOT MUCH HAS CHANGED

Since Bigger Thomas haunted hungry Chi-Town streets
Black boy in search of him black self
Amid heavy prison bars shiny as bling

Supreme Court Justice Thomas still eats pork
White folks still hang nooses from trees
And drag black bodies behind pickup trucks
Along black tar roads bloody with snow

*

Emmett Till was twisted into a tire
Iron and tossed into a black river
For staring at Mary Dalton too long

Bigger Thomas rose out of that bog
And put a white pillow to her
White face until it turned as pale
As the bones in the Atlantic Ocean

*

Hip Hop's Bigger Thomas in a hoody
On trial for killing white peoples' dreams
Of OJ finally behind bars—Supreme schemes

That date back to nose broke Sphinx
Break dancing on *La Amistad* ship deck
Hanged between pyramids and prisons like scare
Crow crowded corners' trapped gold tooth grimace

We all sat around reading a book
They Burn Witches, Don't They?

Oh a blanket full of hives
    A blanket full of hives
Hi Ho America
    A blanket full of hives
(Poem song)

I am The Taliban of Love
I will terrorize your thighs

Early American suicide bombers
Strapped measles & smallpox
To blankets
Sent them to reservations
Along with bottles of 100 proof
In exchange for land

Became a major motion picture
Dances with Real Estate Agents

They Drop Atomic Bombs, Don't They?

Hiroshima Nagosaki
Here's a piece of my Gestopi
Uranium for your cranium
Plutonium for your bootonium

Columbus came w/ bibles & bayonets
Slicing ears slitting nostrils
The vile pestilence of imperial aggression
In the shadow of Jesus burning on a cross,
The Good Ship Lollipop
W/ conquistadors & moors
Wanting more
What a bore it would be
To just collect gold & silver
& Indian scalps—
Must have bodies—plenty
Of bodies: black brown yellow & blue

To fuck & breed
To work to death for
Profit & greed
To civilize & indoctrinate
To steal & hate—seal all fate

We did not wait we did not wait
For blue grass blues or R&B
For country music polka lessons
Or jazz CDs
To paint a portrait of a world gone mad
With contradictions

Contrary to popular opinion
Death was always the prescription

Here is the first & foremost mandate:

Steal the land
Pack their mouths with sand
Slap on a toe tag & brand
Fit for a body bag & scag
Fit for a noose or biddy
Fit for electric chairs
Of refried beans left
In your smoldering pants

Eyebrows singed & shrunken brain
Collapsed & broken
The heart explodes & splatters
In the caged ribs of lungs
Filled with lethal gas & fluid

The eyes are blank slates
The nape crushed like a grape
The back a launching pad
Of hysterical cries

While history books & TV
Continue to lie
Prostrate on the ground,
The cop says, kicking
Your teeth
In.

Uhm, yummy
Like candy corn trick o' treat or
Jelly beans & lemon heads
You swallow each one
'Til you gum your last gasp of air
& a gun is planted
In the cracked clay pot
Of your open skull

This is the part where the choir
Comes in—

We shall O vuh cu uh um
     We shall O vuh cu uh um
We shall O vuh cu uh um
     Some day

Your ship will come in
it will be called The Niña The Pinta
The Santa María
It will be called Jesus & Mary
& Freedom

It will be big enough to fit your entire
Genetic line of DNA
Laid spoon style
In a glove compartment
Of shit & piss in a
Bucket of afterbirth & snot
It will be called—The Love Boat

A welcoming committee
Will corral you & yours
W/ rope & noose w/ ankle chains & lash
Your neighbors will greet you
With burning crosses on your front lawn
Roast marshmallows of your first born
Separate you & your loved ones
Like church & state
Make geometric use of your skin
Lampshades & baseball mitts
Industrial soaps & museum memorabilia
For your kin

So much will be made
Of your contribution
To humanity
So much will be made
Of your hiney

Mass graves & museums
Concentration camp mausoleums
Slave castles & hulls of ships
Bones line the bottom of the sea
From Teotihuacán to Wounded Knee
From Africa to Cherokee
Bones line the bottom of the sea

KWANSABA

for Eugene B. Redmond

Memory is a burden you carry bold
Like braille whip maps on your back
A mouth full of sand and mud
At the bottom of oceans bloated with
Bones gnawed at by seaweed and time
Memory is a pool of blood ringing
Like seashell swirl in your inner ear

BIRTHIN' BLUES BY THE BAYOU

for Kalamu ya Salaam

Nobody loves me but my mother
and she could be jivin' too.
                    —B.B. King

I have been hungry
Before you came

My forehead cannot
Stand the stain

What sticks is what
We remember

High watermarks
On the chin

Broke ribcage bones
Whistling in the wind

Who cares if all I have to eat is
Dust and pigeon wings

What don't kill you
Will make you sing

Acknowledgments

Grateful acknowledgment is made to the publishers and editors of the following publications where these poems previously appeared, some in slightly different form:

Say It Loud! Poems about James Brown edited by Mary Weems and Michael Oatman (Whirlwind Press, 2011): "JB's Great Escape" and "Brown Sonnet"

Spaces Between Us: Poetry, Prose and Art on HIV/AIDS edited by Kelly Norman Ellis and M.L. Hunter (Third World Press, 2010): "Francine Francis (age 13)" and "Chucha's Last Christmas"

Full Moon on K Street: Poems about Washington, DC edited by Kim Roberts (Plan B Press, 2010): "Cannibals on U Street"

Let Loose on the World: Celebrating Amiri Baraka at 75 edited by Ted Wilson, et al. (The Amiri Baraka Commemoration Committee, 2009): "Serious Trouble Will Bypass You"

Poets Against the Killing Fields edited by Tontongi, Jill Netchinsky and Brenda Walcott, et al. (Trilingual Press, 2007): "Questions on the Police Officer's Exam"; "An Onion of Wars"; "Bread"; "Los Olvidados"; "Lebanon"; "Camden"; "Congo" and "Gaza Stripped"

Little Patuxten Review (Issue 11, Social Justice Issue, 2012): "Barack Obama (age 50)"

Drumvoices Revue (20th Anniversary Issue, 2012): "Kwansaba"

Bureau 39 edited by Lesley-Ann Brown (Bandit Queen Press, 2011): "Things to Blame Hip Hop For"

Words, Beat & Life: "Things to Blame Hip Hop For" and "Bestseller, Required Text, the Future of Black Literature?"

phati'tude Literary Magazine (Volume 2, Number 4); *Celebrating Black History Through Literature: From the Harlem Renaissance to Today*: "Hip Hop Hurts Sometimes"

The Journal of Pan African Studies (Volume 4, Number 2, December 2010): "On Laura Schlessinger and Her N-Word Rant"; "Everything You Wanted to Know about Hip Hop but Were Afraid to Be Hipped for Fear of Being Hopped" and "Slam-A-Lot"

Amistad (Fall/Winter 2010): "Rumsfeld Confesses at a Mosque in Harlem"

Reverie: Midwest African American Literature (Volume 4, 2010): "Red" and "Blue Scowl Aubade"

Tidal Basin Review (Volume 1, Number 2, August 2010): "Lydia Muñoz (age 13)" and "Samantha Negrón (age 13)"

Tidal Basin Review (Volume 1, Number 1, April 2010): "When I Think of You, Love"; "First Suit" and "Star"

Paterson Literary Review (PLR) # 37 (2009): "Broke Barbie" and "An Onion of Wars"

Columbia Poetry Review (No. 21, Spring 2008): "Los Olvidados"

Drumvoices Revue (Spring-Summer-Fall 2008, Volume 16, Numbers 1 & 2): "Alas, Poor Richard, Not Much Has Changed"

Scarab (Anansi, 2006): "Autobiography of a Welfano"; "Byrd on a Wire" and "Gaza Stripped"

WarpLand: A Journal of Black Literature and Ideas (Volume 12, Number 1, 2005): "The Autobiography of Michael Jackson's Skin"

I would like to express my gratitude to everyone who made this book possible: My publisher, Dr. Haki R. Madhubuti; my editor Gwendolyn Mitchell; Miriam Ahmed, who created such a great cover and book design; the Third World Press family: Rose Perkins, Bennett Johnson, Catherine Compton, Relana Johnson and anyone else at TWP I neglected to mention. I would also like to thank my colleague, Kitty Ellison, my student, Shakeema Smalls, and Alexa Muñoz for their keen eyes. I'd be remiss if I did not thank my creative writing students at Howard University who read through an earlier version of this book in manuscript form as I attempted to order these poems. Lastly, I'd like to give a special thanks to my heroes in art and struggle: Nikki Giovanni, Jan Carew, Haile Gerima and Amiri Baraka.

Bio

Tony Medina was born in the South Bronx and spent much of his adult life living in Harlem. The author/editor of sixteen books for adults and young readers, Medina is a two-time winner of the Paterson Prize for Books for Young People for *DeShawn Days* (2001) and *I and I, Bob Marley* (2009). His anthology, *Bum Rush the Page: A Def Poetry Jam*, was a *Washington Post* Best Book of the Year (2001). Medina's latest collections of poetry include *The President Looks Like Me, Broke on Ice* and *My Old Man Was Always on the Lam*, a finalist for the 2011 Paterson Poetry Prize. An advisory editor for Nikki Giovanni's *Hip Hop Speaks to Children*, he is featured in the poetry documentary *Furious Flower II* and the *Encyclopedia of Hip Hop Literature*. Medina, who holds an MA and PhD from Binghamton University, is the first-ever Professor of Creative Writing at Howard University. He has read his work, lectured and conducted workshops extensively across the country and abroad. His poetry, fiction and essays appear in over ninety anthologies and publications, and he is the author and editor of two previous Third World Press titles, *Committed to Breathing* (2003) and *Role Call* (2002).

Praise for An Onion of Wars

Tony Medina is what a poet should be: Brave. Eyes are suppose to see; hearts are required to feel; and hands hold that beautiful, fragile thing…Integrity. No juggling act; no balancing. Brave, strong, wonderful to read a poet who loves enough to offend; who laughs at his own foibles; who takes our hand and leads us to the magic of peeling and peeling and peeling until we find the truth and the light. *An Onion of Wars* takes us to new places. Read and be renewed.

— **Nikki Giovanni** | author of *Bicycles: Love Poems*

The poetry of Tony Medina is complex. It strips the street to its simplest common denominator of survival and tears off layer upon layer of stark realism. Behind every episode is a poetic imagination piecing together shards of light and darkness on the minutia of survival against daunting odds. This is a peerless social and political document. A commentary on the contemporary social scene, it is well-researched and there is an absence of the ego-tripping to which so many social commentators fall victim. And, like all good poetry, there are memorable lines that will remain with you long after you have put the book down.

— **Jan Carew** | author of *The Guyanese Wanderer*

In his new book of poetry, *An Onion of Wars*, Tony Medina continues to be a poet with an individual voice of his own, without compromising the collective tradition of liberation voices, which makes his poetry a voice of a unique revolutionary. Often we wonder and agonize trying to envision a generational transaction for our respective artistic expressions. Tony not only nurtures future poets, he gives validation to their own unique and individual voices, bringing them along in the onion of wars and setting in motion cadres of future warrior poets. In *An Onion of Wars* I can't help but see and hear the continuity of poetic voices of visionary greats like Sterling Brown, Gwendolyn Brooks, Haki Madhubuti, Amiri Baraka, John Coltrane and Sonia Sanchez.

— **Haile Gerima** | writer and director of *Sankofa and Teza*

411-BAC-546

Tony Medina's poetry is as hard as the ey… …lentlessly expressive of historic and contemporary rage — plus it is funny… …switchblade of laughter jugging you, and with that, revelation!

— **Amiri Baraka** | author of *Digging: T… …ul of American Classical Music*

$18

ISBN 978-0-88378-330-6

51895

9 780883 783306

P8-ALG-768

Third World Press
www.twpbooks.com